For I will consider my Cat Jeoffry …

'Wittily and deftly imagined … Jeoffry is the
greatest cat in the English language'
Hilary Mantel

'Beautifully written, wise and wonderfully
entertaining'
Andrew O'Hagan

'Both playful and profound: it's a little classic.
I found it tremendously moving'
Eileen Atkins

'Simply unforgettable … This is a book to savour,
reflect upon, and give to friends'
Alexander McCall Smith

'Ravishing … A lovely little book'
Min Wild, *TLS*

'Soden's delightful, insinuating book curls around
your thoughts and tickles you with its whiskers'
Laura Freeman, *The Economist*

T0008506

Jeoffry was a real cat who lived 250 years ago, confined to an asylum with Christopher Smart, one of the most visionary poets of the age. In exchange for love and companionship, Smart rewarded Jeoffry with the greatest tribute to a feline ever written.

Prize-winning biographer Oliver Soden combines meticulous research with passages of dazzling invention to recount the life of the cat praised as 'a mixture of gravity and waggery'. The narrative roams from the theatres and bordellos of Covent Garden to the cell where Smart was imprisoned for mania. At once whimsical and profound, witty and deeply moving, Soden's biography plays with the genre like a cat with a toy. It tells the story of a poet and a poem, while setting Jeoffry's life and adventures against the roaring backdrop of eighteenth-century London.

PRAISE FOR *JEOFFRY*

gentle. It is full of historical detail and whimsy, in more or less equal measure. It is a complete treat ... a lovely, enchanting piece of work'

Alexander McCall Smith, author of *The No. 1 Ladies' Detective Agency*

'An absolute classic ... Soden combines the originality of wit and concept found in Virginia Woolf's *Flush* with an intimate portrayal of the humanity of a cat that T.S. Eliot understood so well. I found myself so gloriously moved and entertained by Jeoffry, who has leapt purring and stretching, hunting and curling his way into my heart'

Juliet Nicolson, author of *A House Full of Daughters*

'In *Jeoffry: The Poet's Cat*, Oliver Soden has pulled off a difficult feat. His book about the life and adventures of Christopher Smart's considerable cat is charming without being twee, light but not lightweight, inventive within the bounds of respect for history ... Beautifully conceived and done with wit and tenderness. A book to cherish in times when Smart's madhouse seems close to home'

Daniel Karlin, *TLS* Books of the Year

'Both playful and profound: it's a little classic. I found it tremendously moving ... You don't have to be a cat lover to like this book – it's about life'

Eileen Atkins on BBC Radio 4's *A Good Read*

'Soden's delightful, insinuating book curls around your thoughts and tickles you with its whiskers ... Soden jokes that if *Jubilate Agno* is a magnificat (a song of praise to God), the Jeoffry verses are a magnifi-cat. His own magnifi-cat recreation … would make a fine stocking filler – silk, buckled or gartered'

Laura Freeman, *The Economist*

'Oliver Soden has done for Christopher Smart's cat Jeoffry what Virginia Woolf did for the Brownings' dog, Flush. Except he's made a much better job of it. This is a beautifully written, wise and wonderfully entertaining account of loyalty and the meaning of biography. Smart's cat was indeed a magical being, and Oliver Soden has plucked a wealth of literary art from the cat's life and from Smart's unforgettable vision. I intend to give a copy to everybody I like'

Andrew O'Hagan, author of *Mayflies*

'A heart-lifting delight; I absolutely loved it. A triumph'

Alexandra Harris, author of *Weatherland*

'Protagonist of the most anthologised section of the mad poet Christopher Smart's *Jubilate Agno*, the eccentrically spelled ginger tom now takes a fresh lease of fictionalised life in this *jeu d'esprit* … It's at once a sly introduction to Christopher Smart and the literary milieu of 18th-century London … and a cat's-eye view of 18th-century social history … It has a good deal, too, to tell the reader about cats … But it also poses the implicit question of how fictional biographies are in any case … All biographies adopt points of view, make suppositions, put fictional flesh on the bones of the facts the record gives us; and their test is how persuasively they do so. This one does so with great panache and not a little of the writerly flourish'

'An intensely poignant portrait of a celebrated cat ... told with vibrant pace and energy ... As we follow the irresistible subject towards and through his interaction with the poet who would give him his immortality, we smell the streets and the confined spaces, we suffer the blows, we weep the tears. This beautifully written and highly affecting book is a must-read for lovers of poetry, of the 18th century, and of cats'

'Soden's clever and vivid book is an imagined biography of this undocumented creature of the London streets ... Jeoffry's life is envisioned here with ingenuity and tact ... Soden can write and knows feline liquidity and transformation'

'Although Jeoffry has become famous through Smart's much-anthologised poem "My Cat Jeoffry", he has left no other pawprint on the historical record ... It is this gap that Oliver Soden proceeds to plug in his delightful "biography" of Jeoffry ... In a particularly fine evocation of a cat's-eye view, Soden has Jeoffry distinguish Smart's asylum visitors from each other by the shape of their lower legs: he is able to tell apart the bulging calves and hobbled feet of Dr Johnson and the more springy limbs of Charles Burney. When David Garrick arrives, Jeoffry recognises him from the way the actor's theatrical vibrato moves the air in the little cell. It is, after all, what whiskers are for'

Kathryn Hughes, *Literary Review*

'A bracing and heartfelt scamper through Georgian London, and the life of a much-loved cat – like Jeoffry himself, this delightful book is an irresistible mixture of "gravity and waggery". With its supporting cast of 18th-century luminaries such as Handel, Dr Johnson and the bloated brothel-keeper Mother Douglas, this is a carefully researched and beautifully imagined feline biography'

Emily Brand, author of *The Fall of the House of Byron*

'Inspired by *Flush*, Virginia Woolf's "biography" of Elizabeth Barrett Browning's dog, Soden's book is a witty, charming, semi-fictional biography of the cat that kept Smart company in the madhouse'

Tristram Fane Saunders, *Daily Telegraph*

'*Jeoffry: The Poet's Cat* is an engrossing recreation of 18th-century London at its grittiest, from brothels to insane asylums, as seen through the eyes of a famous cat. The blend of scrupulous scholarship with imaginative invention is wonderfully effective'

Leo Damrosch, author of *The Club*

'I greatly enjoyed this book ... Oliver Soden has found a really vivid "ground-level" way to capture Georgian

London, and as soon as Smart comes on the scene a most moving chemistry develops between the cat who has no words and the poet who is adrift in them'

Ann Wroe, author of *Francis*

A masterpiece of witty and learned speculative biography'

Daunt Books

'A beautiful picture of a cat [but] the book is as much about Christopher Smart. Heartbreaking … I had a lump in my throat and I don't often cry at books … I learned so much from it'

Harriett Gilbert on BBC Radio 4's *A Good Read*

Jeoffry
The Poet's Cat

OLIVER SODEN

For Ruth Smith

First published 2020
This paperback edition published 2022
Reprinted 2023

The History Press
97 St George's Place, Cheltenham,
Gloucestershire, GL50 3QB
www.thehistorypress.co.uk

British Library Cataloguing in Publication Data.
A catalogue record for this book is available from the British Library.

ISBN 978 0 7509 9931 1

Typesetting and origination by The History Press
Printed and bound in Great Britain by TJ Books Limited, Padstow, Cornwall

Trees for LYfe

"CAT. n.s. [katz, Teuton. Chat, Fr.] A domestick animal that catches mice, commonly reckoned by naturalists the lowest order of the leonine species."

Samuel Johnson, *A Dictionary of the English Language*, Vol. I

"[Christopher Smart's] poem about his cat is to all other poems about cats what the *Iliad* is to all other poems on war."

T.S. Eliot, "Walt Whitman and Modern Poetry"

"All faiths, whether religious, humanistic, instinctive, or the creative artist's act of praise, are in fact one."

Patrick White, *Letters*

CONTENTS

AUTHOR'S NOTE

This book is a biography of Jeoffry, the real-life cat who belonged to the poet Christopher Smart (1722–71).

Between 1759 and 1763, and partly while incarcerated in an asylum with only Jeoffry for company, Smart wrote his vast religious poem *Jubilate Agno* (*Rejoice in the Lamb*). The poem was not published until 1939, after fragments of the manuscript were discovered in a private library.

Jeoffry gave rise to the most famous section of the poem: "For I will consider my Cat Jeoffry …". These seventy-four lines of verse are among the most anthologised poetry in the language. In 1943 they were further immortalised in a musical setting by Benjamin Britten.

The dividing line between fact and fiction in this biography is necessarily wobbly, and sometimes one is disguised as the other. Had the facts survived, I would have written them. I have tried never to invent where information is known.

The extant text of *Jubilate Agno* can be found most easily in *Christopher Smart: Selected Poems* (London: Penguin, 1990). The poem's 1,739 lines – all that survive of an estimated 4,000 – are divided into four fragments: A, B, C, and D. The seventy-four lines devoted to Jeoffry are B695–768.

THE POEM

For I will consider my Cat Jeoffry.

For he is the servant of the Living God duly and daily serving him.

For at the first glance of the glory of God in the East he worships in his way.

For this is done by wreathing his body seven times round with elegant quickness.

For then he leaps up to catch the musk, which is the blessing of God upon his prayer.*

For he rolls upon prank to work it in.

For having done duty and received blessing he begins to consider himself.

For this he performs in ten degrees.

For first he looks upon his forepaws to see if they are clean.

For secondly he kicks up behind to clear away there.

For thirdly he works it upon stretch with the forepaws extended.

For fourthly he sharpens his paws by wood.

---

*   Lines marked with an asterisk (*) are discussed in the Notes (pp. 167–71).

For fifthly he washes himself.

For sixthly he rolls upon wash.

For seventhly he fleas himself, that he may not be interrupted upon the beat.*

For eighthly he rubs himself against a post.

For ninthly he looks up for his instructions.

For tenthly he goes in quest of food.

For having consider'd God and himself he will consider his neighbour.

For if he meets another cat he will kiss her in kindness.

For when he takes his prey he plays with it to give it a chance.

For one mouse in seven escapes by his dallying.

For when his day's work is done his business more properly begins.

For he keeps the Lord's watch in the night against the adversary.

For he counteracts the powers of darkness by his electrical skin and glaring eyes.

For he counteracts the Devil, who is death, by
brisking about the life.

For in his morning orisons he loves the sun and the
sun loves him.

For he is of the tribe of Tiger.

For the Cherub Cat is a term of the Angel Tiger.

For he has the subtlety and hissing of a serpent,
which in goodness he suppresses.

For he will not do destruction, if he is well-fed,
neither will he spit without provocation.

For he purrs in thankfulness, when God tells him
he's a good Cat.

For he is an instrument for the children to learn
benevolence upon.

For every house is incompleat without him and a
blessing is lacking in the spirit.

For the Lord commanded Moses concerning the
cats at the departure of the Children of Israel
from Egypt.*

For every family had one cat at least in the bag.*

For the English Cats are the best in Europe.

For he is the cleanest in the use of his forepaws of
any quadruped.

For the dexterity of his defence is an instance of the
love of God to him exceedingly.

For he is the quickest to his mark of any creature.

For he is tenacious of his point.

For he is a mixture of gravity and waggery.

For he knows that God is his Saviour.

For there is nothing sweeter than his peace when
at rest.

For there is nothing brisker than his life when in
motion.

For he is of the Lord's poor and so indeed is he
called by benevolence perpetually—Poor Jeoffry!
poor Jeoffry! the rat has bit thy throat.

For I bless the name of the Lord Jesus that Jeoffry
is better.

For the divine spirit comes about his body to sus-
tain it in compleat cat.

For his tongue is exceeding pure so that it has in
purity what it wants in musick.

For he is docile and can learn certain things.

For he can set up with gravity which is patience upon approbation.

For he can fetch and carry, which is patience in employment.

For he can jump over a stick which is patience upon proof positive.

For he can spraggle upon waggle at the word of command.*

For he can jump from an eminence into his master's bosom.

For he can catch the cork and toss it again.

For he is hated by the hypocrite and miser.

For the former is afraid of detection.

For the latter refuses the charge.

For he camels his back to bear the first notion of business.*

For he is good to think on, if a man would express himself neatly.

For he made a great figure in Egypt for his signal services.

For he killed the Ichneumon-rat very pernicious by land.*

For his ears are so acute that they sting again.*

For from this proceeds the passing quickness of his attention.

For by stroaking of him I have found out electricity.*

For I perceived God's light about him both wax and fire.

For the Electrical fire is the spiritual substance, which God sends from heaven to sustain the bodies both of man and beast.

For God has blessed him in the variety of his movements.

For, tho he cannot fly, he is an excellent clamberer.

For his motions upon the face of the earth are more than any other quadruped.

For he can tread to all the measures upon the musick.

For he can swim for life.

For he can creep.

Christopher Smart, from *Jubilate Agno*
(B695–768)

I

THE CATTERY

1750–1753

The earth shook when Jeoffry was born. Fish jumped out of the river, chimneys rained from the roofs, and the bells clanged in their steeples.

His life began in a cupboard, under the back staircase of a grand house in the Covent Garden Piazza. It was early March 1750. Frock-coated men had left their wigs and their consciences on a small Oriental table by the door, and were losing themselves among the perfumed candlelight of the upper rooms in a whirl of powder and petti-coats. Jeoffry's siblings had been arriving through the night at thirty-minute intervals, but the last kitten seemed reluctant to appear. Suddenly the cupboard was thrown violently from side to side, and a shower of dust fell onto the wriggling family, which squeaked at the sudden roar and clank from the street outside. And Jeoffry was shaken into the world. The beds in the rooms above tipped their couples apart as the house shivered around them and china fell from the dressing tables. A stream of scantily clad people made for the front door, and were not noticed in the piazza, which was already speckled with dozy Londoners clutching at their dressing gowns in the drizzling dawn.

It was the second earthquake to have rocked London that year, and in the weeks that followed, as Jeoffry was slowly accustoming himself to the world, rumours of an impending third began to circulate. Quack doctors did a roaring trade in well-padded "earthquake coats", which sold in their hundreds to a scared public. Through the windows of the bordello came frightened predictions of further destruction. Vicars preached of sin and judgement. Business in the house became slow, and the cats dozed through the frightened days. When the fated hour approached, at least four of the girls began to pack their bags. The cacophony that daily assaulted Jeoffry's slowly lengthening ears grew first noisy and then still. The streets lay abandoned, the straw rotted in empty stables, and the windows of the capital's houses were dark. The cats in the cupboard under the stairs lay barely remembered. Fear settled on the streets like fog. Londoners had gone. Taverns from Blackheath to Islington doubled their rates and placed "full" signs outside their doors. Came the dreaded moment when St Paul's was to have crashed into the metropolis and houses fallen to dust; hundreds of city-dwellers had stuffed themselves onto the barges and boats of the filthy Thames. Young children climbed the rigging while their parents prayed and braced themselves for disaster. The boats rocked under the load, but the city that lay spread out before them did not stir. And so they all went home again.[1]

Jeoffry knew little of the abortive apocalypse, of the mood that spread through the city around him, half relieved at its second chance, half ashamed at its foolishness. In fact he knew little of anything, and his early days were spent in a swaddle of darkness and quiet. His eyes and ears edged themselves safely and slowly into the world, and not until he was three weeks old, still nuzzling into the suedey underside of his mother, did a bright slice of light shoot from the hall of the house beneath the ill-fitting cupboard door and in through a small crack in his six eyelids. (As with all his species, each of his eyes was thrice lidded.)

The distant fugue of Covent Garden reached Jeoffry's cupboard, and made his brothers and sisters – seven or eight of them, it seems – stretch and flex their tiny claws. Strange noises, later terrifying to him, were made safe by their unfamiliarity, as dogs barked and howled, and carriages trundled past, and market sellers yelled their wares, stacked their produce, bartered with customers. It was a chorus of laughter and tears and shouting, with a harsh descant provided by the ladies of the house, who would beckon passers-by into the rooms whose floorboards squeaked and thudded above Jeoffry's head.

What is known of his ancestry can be swiftly narrated. Rather than growing into his colouring, Jeoffry was born in his coat, a fuzz of carrot and his progeny well. In fact, he lay in a scrape of fur and blood at the side of Hart (now Floral) Street, dashed beneath the wheels of a speeding carriage during an ill-judged scurry. Jeoffry's mother, too, exhausted by her latest brood of demanding and mewling kittens, which were piled beneath her in a mass of ginger and tortoiseshell and calico, the smallest yowling and born lacking its tail, the largest champing at her with angry gums, slipped first into an exhausted sleep and then into a peaceful death, still lying in the wooden crate under the stairs that she had singled out for herself a few weeks into her last pregnancy. She was found, kept warm amid the clump and squirm of her children, by the prettiest and most popular of Mother Douglas's ladies, who had rolled her eyes at the earthquake foolishness and stayed put. Nancy Burroughs had picked out Jeoffry's mother (her name is undiscovered) as her own particular favourite and comfort. She had been looking into the cupboard from time to time, snaffling hot towels from the kitchen and providing bowls of milk, and occasionally wiping desultorily at the mess with a pile of rags, lest the cats, who were somehow her special and enduring secret in the turmoil of her life, be discovered and turned out.

Occasionally, on the nights that were her own absolutely, she had allowed Jeoffry's mother to pad tentatively through the perfumed drapery of her room and pour herself up onto the bed, to sleep all night at its foot, a thrumming loaf of warmth. Nancy did not mourn the cat's death. Another client was shortly due whose tastes and rituals took time to prepare, and more pressing was the fact that she now had to deal with a pile of hungry kittens. A quick word was had with a sympathetic cook, who took the tailless runt and drowned it efficiently in the back yard. The rest seemed destined to go the same way, and at least two of them must have done, but Nancy sent word round those women in the house whom she knew the best, and whispers shot along the corridors of Betsys and

Jennys, Pollys and Sallys. One scrabbling ball of tabby found its way out of the house in the velvet pocket of a nervous teenage viscount, who had taken a fancy to the suggestion that he might like a fluffy keepsake of his unsatisfactory deflowering. Nancy paid further snatched visits to the box under the stairs, and lined it as best she could with the scraps of stained muslin that, they had been hurriedly told by a red-faced Mother Douglas, were kept in a special cupboard. She noticed that the kittens had begun to disappear, squirrelled away in the corners of cupboards or under beds, or fed to dogs, or who could say?

She had long noticed the kitten that seemed to keep to himself at the corner of the crate, aimlessly trying to chew the edge of the box with his toothless gums. He mewled in either discontent or pleasure, she couldn't tell, whenever she ran her long forefinger with its painted nail down through the tiger stripes on his back. His fur seemed to shine brighter than the others. This would be her gift to herself; her mascot and her talisman. There had been cats roaming on the grounds of the house where she had grown up, and she had liked watching them howl and hiss, tumbling over and over each other in lust or rage or play. They had not been cats for stroking or loving, and her world had had space for neither, but this one might be a beacon of affection, given and received, in an uncherished life. One night she slipped down to the cupboard door and cupped her hands around his scrabbling paws, which soon speckled her wrists with a bracelet of red beads. She got him into a silk stocking, and carried him back up to her room.

He was not called Jeoffry, then, and Nancy appears to have given him the rather unfortunate name of Squit, or even Squits (the handwriting of her surviving diaries is often illegible). The name was presumably a reference to his size or to his digestive trouble. Cats are, after all, lactose intolerant, and the kitten appears to have been surviving on a diet of bread and milk. But to avoid my readers' confusion and my subject's indignity he will be referred to as Jeoffry throughout. He did not see his brothers and sisters again (their fates are unknown), nor the cupboard that had formed the limits of his world.

Weeks and months were foreign divisions to him. Time was lived moment by moment, divided into a speedily worked-out ritual of the light hours and the dark. He did not know himself motherless, so did not miss his mother, but the absence of the training she might have instilled, the world of safety and cleanliness she would have created for him, soon made itself felt. He huddled in a ball of nerves, and Nancy cursed her decision and her third-floor room as she vainly put together a box of piled straw that he declined to use for his toilet, preferring a clump of long-forgotten skirts that lay soiled under the bed. She washed them as best she could late at night, fearing people would think the mess hers, and when Jeoffry eventually took to the straw box she cleaned that in the night too, drenching the room with perfume afterwards and coming rather to enjoy the solitary ritual.

When clients arrived Nancy shoved him, ungainly, beneath the bed, and somehow he knew he was not to emerge. His view became obscured by piles of clothes and shoes, and he pressed himself up against the cool china of the chamber pot, an edifice of impossible vastness and strange scent, and he watched with unimpressed amber gaze the strange counterpoint of feet that waved and tangled down by the side of the bed. The tops of Nancy's were soft and painted, but her soles and heels were calloused and yellow. Above them thick ankles and hairy toes dabbled and probed. In the darkness, Jeoffry would track the thick-ridged mustard toenails with his eyes, tail switching. Occasionally, as Nancy's mind drifted, she thought she heard the ginger swish beneath the slats of the bedframe, the clatter of claws on the floorboards as he pounced at a chemise or gnawed at a corset bone. Once, he had torn out from under the bed while a gentleman was dressing, nearly giving a heart attack to the old regular who, afterwards, sitting on the chaise longue with his shirt-tails lapping at his pale thighs, did not see the joke. When it happened again, to a younger man with a wine-splash birthmark spread around one eye, Jeoffry was taken in good humour and petted. And when it happened a third time, to a bald man who for a guinea's surcharge would place his hard hands around Nancy's neck and squeeze until she gasped, he stamped on the end of Jeoffry's tail in bad temper, storming out never to return.

The man's rage had blown open the door, and Jeoffry skimmed out before him, screeching, and sped down the empty corridor. Finding no escape, he arched his back, made a harsh noise of fear and pain, and then curled into a tight ball of defensive fury and pushed his nose into the grubby green of the skirting board. The man shot down the stairs, still shouting, and later Mother Douglas would upbraid Nancy for whatever had gone on, slapping with an angelic mouth and blond curls who did what and as he was told and on whom many of them had rather doted, became quite incensed by the four-legged arrival. His mother, Mrs Craft, saved scraps from the kitchen and enjoyed shooing Jeoffry away from the food and out of the back door. The fun came in their uniting against Mother Douglas; Jeoffry had become their rebellion. She had glimpsed him once or twice, on the few occasions that she hobbled, bloated and breathless, up to the top floors of the house, and he had got beneath the mound of her skirts. "Get that filthy cat out of here," she had said, and they had said they would, and didn't. Lustrous in her youth, a canny businesswoman with an eye for spotting beautiful girls and the rich men who might bed them, she had made this, her second establishment, one of the most opulent in London, and Jeoffry wandered beneath gilt-framed paintings and heard the novel clank and bubble of water running down the newly installed pipework behind the hand-painted defend London from the second Jacobite rebellion. (Had Nancy ever seen the painting, she would have recognised Mr Hogarth's satire for what it was, knowing how very impious Mother Douglas could be.) And on the roof of the bordello, so high in the top right-hand corner of the picture that they seem to be making a beeline for the safety of its frame, sit three cats, displaying the contempt for acrophobia shared by most of their species. Or at least they share, if Jeoffry is any evidence of typical feline behaviour, a happy disregard for getting up to high places. *Getting down* is another matter. They display too a contempt for the viewer, the third offering nothing but a rude flash of his rear end, as if emulating the behaviour he was used to witnessing from the women at the windows below.

Mr Hogarth paints in the vocabulary of the satirist: a careful viewer would need no Georgian crib-sheet to work out what a "cattery" might be. Yet, doubtless, the artist had seen just such a cat as Jeoffry, perhaps his father, perhaps a distant relation, slinking around the corners of Mother Douglas's catteries, and was painting from life, as well as painting in code. The cats in others of Hogarth's works appear on street-signs hanging outside bordellos, or snuffling beneath the crinolines of his fallen women. They are incarcerated, as Nancy and her compatriots were; a personification of a harlot, but also a harlot's companion, her *daemon*, as any ermine might be to a grand lady by da Vinci. The hideous treatment of cats in Hogarth's *The Four Stages of Cruelty* or other, earlier, paintings form a reminder of just how novel Nancy's adoption of Jeoffry as a pet actually was. But to keep and to feed an animal with and for pleasure was an activity becoming more and more common in Georgian England: witness Hogarth's *The Graham Children*, in which the family pet appears not on a lap but behind a high-backed chair, staring with lamplit eyes and horrible focus at a caged goldfinch – and stealing the viewer's attention all but completely, like an ill-disciplined actor in a chorus.

Jeoffry's ancestors had been mousers, scavengers, strays, emaciated and ravenous, roaming the streets mangy with disease. They had danced around the witches' bonfire at midnight and dodged stones from an angry crowd. They had gone to sea with the navy, swiping at rats below deck; they had mewed longingly at seabirds, with salt spray in their whiskers; they had died slowly, of starvation, in the corner of a stinking hull, or speedily, from storm or cannon fire, in a booming crack of wood and a terrifying wall of water.

Jeoffry knew none of these things, as, over the years, he grew to love and to appreciate not only food and warmth and softness, but the affectionate and work-worn hands that provided all three. Zooming briefly up and away from Covent Garden, leaving Jeoffry in a purring slumber of bedsheet and content, we might consider a map of Georgian London dotted with the country's new phenomenon: the domesticated feline, *Felis catus*, carnivorous, furry, suffering the indignity of being dressed and petted by the young ladies of their households, and peering with a well-fed superiority through sash windows onto their feral friends in the filthy street below. Horace Walpole – man of letters, Whig politician – sits in his father's house in Arlington Street in St James's, with his handsome tabby, Zara, and remembers with a brisk grief the death of Zara's companion, Selima, who, batting at some goldfish drifting aimless but tantalising in a china bowl, had tumbled into the water and drowned, to be immortalised, shortly afterwards, in Thomas Gray's "Ode on the Death of a Favourite Cat". In an attic room at Southwark, a black kitten nicknamed Hodge frolics around the hooped dresses of two women who wonder whether the cat might not eventually be a good companion for a literary gentleman they know who is mourning the recent death of his wife and seems generally in a bad way. And Jeoffry, coming up to his third birthday, dozes in the velveteen arms of Nancy, in a beautifully furnished room on the third floor of Mother Douglas's whorehouse, on the north-eastern corner of Covent Garden Piazza.

Jeoffry spent most of the nights under the bed, and much of the day – as the months went on – galloping round the bedroom and trying to jump up at the window with his white-gloved front paws. Days and nights were arbitrary divisions in Nancy's life, many of her clients being nocturnal. Her mornings were spent half-asleep, cursing Jeoffry for attempting to scrabble up the curtains. Once she caught him hanging off the thick shawls that she had wound around the curtain pole to keep out the morning sunshine. She lived in perpetual fear of his somehow throwing himself out of an open window, but he never managed to do more than launch himself at the wall about three feet below the glass. Tables and wardrobes towered above him; these were to be climbed, and he climbed them, or tried to, carving rivulets into the veneer, and flaying the crimson corners of the faded chaise longue. Terrible for him was the day when he gained courage to scramble up and onto the carved splendour of her dressing table, in the process upsetting a glass jar that scattered small pills in a pattering shower across the floor. Only for a moment could he dance joyfully amid them, as Nancy, on the verge of tears, kicked him away and scrambled to save and gather what she could. Mother Douglas set great store by the availability of her *pillules*, which could be administered to any client who complained of soreness or was found to be raw and clammy with rash. They were expensive to obtain, and Nancy would be expected to replace any lost supplies from her own wages.

Chief among Jeoffry's toys, much to Nancy's annoyance and delight, were the condoms that she kept on her dressing table in silk bags tied with ribbon, and which were sometimes strewn across the thickly carpeted floor, left where some hasty baronet had discarded them, and waiting for rinsing and re-use. They were too costly to waste, even for the ladies of Mother Douglas's establishment, who were told in no uncertain terms to make sure the items were available and could be applied with dextrous speed. None of this was of consequence to Jeoffry, who delighted in chasing the sticky sheaths around the floor and found they flopped and squirmed delightfully beneath his paws and nose, as he detected but did not recognise the strange cacophony of scents that throbbed from the animal-skin wrappings, sulphurous and faintly acrid. In exasperation Nancy had to examine every inch of them for the pin-prick holes of Jeoffry's play-ful claws, and learned to check if each would still inflate like a balloon prior to a client's visit. Those that did not she often used anyway, knowing it was the novelty rather than the efficacy of the item that appealed to her gentlemen.

Later, she would make her own arrangements with a makeshift cannula, steaming in front of the fire in a tin bath, having heated the water more than she could really bear. Jeoffry hauled himself up to look over the edge and bat at the soap bubbles, turning on her that disapproving feline gaze that can manage to seem at once voyeuristic and prudish. And if the bath, weeks later, proved not to have worked, she knew to keep her gaze inscrutable as the apothecary handed her the familiar sachet in its brown paper bag, and had grown almost used to the bitter powder it contained, and the stabbing hours of cramp that would follow, her skirts hoiked over a bucket in the privacy of her room. Crawling into the cold bed, she would long for Jeoffry to leap up beside her. Often he did, and she would trail her long fingers through his rippling fur, as if dangling them over the side of a boat in summer to skim through the warm water. He looked at her with his quizzical eyes, which were shaped like almonds and coloured like hazelnuts, and pushed his chill nose into the space between her knuckles, and frisked his whiskers over the chipped varnish on her nails. Marching territorially and pounding the quilt, he purred articulately and then arranged himself into a crescent of knowing elegance at her side. Nancy

2

THE RAID

1753–1759

Living more openly in the house, growing older and larger, Jeoffry had access to the outside world. The bundle of straw that had been his toilet, the scrap of glass that had been his glimpse of sky, had begun to cede to the infinite possibilities, the boundless realms, of the flagstones in the backyard. Freedom, escape, release. Jeoffry was entranced. His nose was growing into itself, his teeth sharpening, and his eyes were wide open, reflecting in their dilations of discovery what to Mother Douglas's ladies was a small courtyard surrounded by a high wall, and what to Jeoffry was a kingdom over which, day after day, he exercised a natural tyranny. The establishment was not the type to leave out crumbs for passing birds, but birds had nevertheless passed, skipping along the grimy wall and fluffing themselves on the lower branches of the bedraggled trees that poked over its edge. But soon the yard was a danger zone, not only to birds, who saw at least three of their comrades snatched from the wall by Jeoffry's playful paws, but to squirrels, who jabbered angrily at the ginger threat and, giggling, easily outran their round-eyed pursuer, pelting him with what nuts or debris they could find.

On rainier days Jeoffry would retreat indoors, skimming up the stairs to the highest rooms of the house, although he did not venture into the stuffy and smoky bedrooms of the lowliest maids. Many hours were spent on Nancy's deep windowsill, bundling his ever-lengthening tangle of limbs into the yard of sunlight that arrived on cue after lunch in the summer months. Otherwise he would make his way outside again to feel the heat of the flagstones on his back, to lap from the pools of filthy water that Mrs Craft and her girls would swill from the kitchen door, or to scratch on the privy to elicit the outraged shrieks of anyone within. He saw the world in a two-hundred-degree vista of moving lights and darks, a tingling monochrome of brightness and motion, interrupted by spurts of blue and green. Reds were foreign to him, but so was complete darkness, and at night he prowled round the yard and along the wall, not yet daring to leap down into the hinterland beyond, tracking the symphony of scent that spun itself across the paving stones, as clear to him as a web of coloured lines, each one to be tracked, followed, separated one from the other, understood. Each evening a pock-marked boy whistled his way across the piazza and, standing on the shoulders of his companion, lit the street lamps, some of which flared from Bow Street to shine like a beacon illuminating Jeoffry's domain. The cat became nothing but a frisking tawny shadow, dabbling in oily globules of lamplight as he coiled his way around the yard.

Cats run at a higher temperature than humans, and while Nancy and her fellows bundled themselves in shawls and huddled ever closer to their increasingly meagre fires, muttering crossly at the blaze they knew to be raging in Mother Douglas's private grate, Jeoffry was sitting on the wall of the yard, unperturbed by the icy wind and the way the sky had filled with the white-grey haze that threatens snow. He was at his favourite position at the far end of the wall, pausing occasionally to stare wide-eyed at low-flying crows, but otherwise content to rock gently back and forth. Already his romantic attitude to safety was maturing into a more careful consideration of the world and its dangers, and Mrs Craft had giggled to herself at just how long he had been sitting there, thinking his unknown thoughts. Nonchalantly he suddenly made good his hours-long planning as if on a whim, and tipped himself off the wall and into the street below. Mrs Craft, powdered in flour, saw an inelegant scrabble of hind legs, and wondered briefly if they would ever see him again.

But Jeoffry was crafty. A leafless tree stood at the corner of the wall, and its branches were an easy journey for a determined and curious cat. For a week or so, regular as clockwork, Jeoffry crept cautiously a few steps along the dung-covered route of Hart Street, feeling his raspberry-soft pads sore against the cobbles and moving slowly round the corner into Bow Street, appraising with his ears the noise of the city, and with his eyes the fast-moving shoes of the tradesmen, just starting to stack up their crates and saddle their horses, boasting to each other of the morning's success. It was around midday. The sun was nowhere to be seen. Unsold fruit was piled in alleyways, popping with insects and assaulting Jeoffry's nose with a thickly rank sweetness that he did not quite dare explore. Far above him the wind blew the bleached signs hanging outside the public houses back and forth in creaking symphony. All this was enough to drive him back up the tree and into the grateful familiarity of the yard.

But soon he mustered courage. He moved speedily enough to dodge kicks or stamps from passers-by who were not looking where they were going. It did not take many weeks for him to learn an observant and dodging slink, to snake his way among boots and along gratings, his pads hardening from silk to leather, his lungs assaulted by the acrid London air and by the bursts of meaty smoke that rose from subterranean kitchens. As the evening drew on, female voices called from the windows above. Jeoffry, recognising not only the garish colours of the window curtains but the rhythm and melody of allure, knew that these houses had functions similar to the one in which he lived. He quickly fostered a loyalty to Nancy and her colleagues, becoming distinctly superior about the many bordellos that studded his soon-regular walking route along the Covent Garden streets. Stature prevented him from looking at them down his nose, but he had his own, rather pungent, ways of marking his disdain.

Five minutes' trot along Hart Street and a quick scrabble round a corner brought him into the dense and colourful jostle of Bow Street. As the months scent, familiar and yet horribly foreign, that first alerted him, and he was brave and curious enough to follow it some twenty yards into a side street that quickly revealed a bundle of spitting black fur, from which two hostile eyes stared with quite horrible focus. This was enough to send Jeoffry scampering back to all that was soft and familiar, but when he again came across another of his own kind, he made himself sit still in front of the strange furry entity (a mangy brown moggy of matted fur to which Jeoffry compared his own with smug pleasure), and meet its piercing gaze. Once or twice he had caught himself in Nancy's looking glass without recognition and struck out. It took an effort of will for his adolescent brain to make its slow connection, using a map of smells more than sights, between his own felineness and that of his enemy. His back arched of its own accord; each individual hair on his body stood to attention with an almost pleasurable prickle of fear and intent. For three long seconds the two cats were astonishingly still,

before a flurry of batting forepaws whirred between
them, scored to a yowling duet in a low and gut-
tural register he had not known he possessed.

He won that round, but would not win all
of them. Of dogs, and his encounters with their
noxious enthusiasm or salivating rage, we will not
speak. Nancy, when she had time, fussed around
him as, week after week, he returned to her room
either cocksure and frolicsome, or in a sulking
bundle of bloodied fur and ragged ears. Some time
late in 1753, or early the following year, Nancy made
an entry, undated, in her diary. (Not all the ladies
of Mother Douglas's establishment were born poor,
or born prostitutes. Many were literate, educated.
Fortunes fall fast. Why Nancy, whose diaries prove
her eloquent and canny, fell into the profession
is unknown.)

Mr E— having departed, his morning visita-
tion having been quite awkward, for I was so
tired, and somehow I cannot quite make my

chamber conducive to such activities in sun-
light, dear Sq [i.e. Jeoffry] came and sat in my
lap for some twenty minutes, purring noisily,
& I confess I might have been happy to sit
there until the afternoon, had not wretched K
entered loudly to clean & quite startled dear
Sq from my skirts – he had a sore at his neck
but would not consent to my applying the
white of an egg for more than a few seconds,
& I fear he spent most of the day with his fur
quite clotted with egg – he was in a fearsome
temper with me & all others of the house &
we did not see him until the late e[ve]ning,
when I was occupied with Lord R——, who
drove me quite beyond my patience by insist-
ing I call him Sweet Babe & requiring that
I spank him for having p—d in his napkins.
When I went to retrieve the birch, I saw Kitty
through [the] window, as he glared at me, all

cross patch from the tree. I doubt* he will be shot some fine day by some irritated neighbour, & I shall miss him quite dreadfully, for all his aggravation.

The lustre of Jeoffry's coat was not entirely dimmed by his explorations, but it took an effort of will, from him and from Nancy, to keep it in the condition he liked. Slowly he began to learn the codes of the gang warfare that the cats of Covent Garden waged among the filthy streets; slowly he found his place in the feline hierarchies of the alleyways, knew the bins in which he could scrabble, found which areas were to be avoided and which to be conquered. Awful was the day when Nancy, in a vague effort to keep him from bringing her what was left of the night's pickings, and to stop him from carrying in birds that were only half-dead and would quickly revive in the warmth of her room,

---

* In the sense of "fear" or "suspect".

spattering the curtains in their fear and knocking into the windows, tied round his neck a pink ribbon threaded through a little bell that she had pulled from one of her more ornamental outfits. It took Jeoffry three days, during which he stayed indoors, sulking, to scratch and tug his way through the ghastly adornment. Only then did he dare to go back outdoors, dignity restored.

Not long afterwards, an observer would have noticed his kittenish high jinks changing perceptibly into a seemingly focused stalking of various trails of scent, to which he added the occasional acrid spray of his own. Not all the cats he came across in the streets of Covent Garden were male, and to the hind quarters of those who allowed him to approach unmolested he paid especial olfactory attention. But let us leave him temporarily in whichever ill-lit and sooty alleyway he has chosen to fight without mercy for his mating rights, in unconscious echo of the transactional activities that were going on in the rooms above his head.

Biographers are often accused of being obsessed with their subjects' sex lives; let us say merely that, given the improbability of Jeoffry's ever having been neutered, it is likely that he roamed ever more far and wide in his consuming wanderlust, and over the years unknowingly speckled the city with wriggling broods of ginger and tortoiseshell.

His wanderings eventually took him to the end of Bow Street, and he padded his way along the taverns and coffee houses of Russell Street, and dared the frightening reek of Drury Lane and its film of coal dust on the air. Certain publicans began to mark the hours by his appearances, and grew quite worried on those days when he had been accidentally locked in Nancy's room and did not appear. The demeanour of the tough alley cat soon ceded to an expansive purr if a saucer of milk or plate of scraps seemed likely to appear from any locals who stooped to pet him. He found a quiet corner on the join between Catherine and Russell Streets where he would usually settle undisturbed each afternoon. Jeoffry came to know one green-gloved hand quite well as it stooped to pet him on its regular arrival from its carriage, haloed by a frothing white cuff, and hovering above a thickly stockinged leg. The owner of the gloved hand had a voice that was rich and resonant, and although Jeoffry understood almost nothing of what was said to him, he felt the low timbre of the voice resonate pleasurably at the fingertips and along his whiskers. The nuzzle from the hand each afternoon became one of Jeoffry's routines, and he was really rather irritated on the days when a higher, whinier voice seemed, in calling away the glove – "Mr Garrick, sir, we really must be moving along!" – to curtail their already brief communion.

On the glove's disappearance, Jeoffry would settle and each afternoon appraise with his beady unblinking stare the crowds of people he did not know to be theatregoers, arriving in their sedan chairs and carriages, and swarming into a side street to attend performances at the Theatre Royal,

Drury Lane, in clouds of ruffles and frills, hoops and swords, high wigs and lemony powder. He watched the coachmen mill around and spit onto the road, the bearers of the sedan chairs stretch their limbs and wipe their brows and scuffle among themselves like any cat. His ears would reach their way towards the distant muffle of laughter and applause, the bang of backstage scenery and yells of stage crew. It was common for audiences to make a single evening's entertainment by taking in an act from an opera here, an act from a play there, moving from theatre to opera house and back again before going on to an afterpiece at the Lincoln's Inn Fields. Jeoffry would watch the crowds moving back and forth until he knew it was time to leave his own ringside seat and return to Mother Douglas's house for a few snatched moments with Nancy before the next of the night's clients returned.

He was a fickle creature, and on other excursions he began to set up camp by the stage door of the Theatre Royal in Covent Garden, unaware of or unbothered by the severe rivalry between the two playhouses. Doorkeepers in both began to boast of how well-trained was their theatre's cat, which they took to be a good-luck charm for sales. Jeoffry was happy to wander over to be scratched or petted, listening with half an ear to the swaddled trumpeting of orchestra or choir. The fingers of the doorkeeper at the Covent Garden theatre were ridged and swollen, marbled with a rough brown growth that scratched pleasantly at Jeoffry's ears. "The takings for your oratorio this evening were quite splendid, Mr Handel," he would say, as Jeoffry saw a pair of swollen legs make their unsteady way up the two steps and into the waiting carriage. "We do believe that this kitten here has had a wonderful effect on the attendance. We've named him Samson, in your honour!"* Jeoffry ducked beneath a cane, had a vague impression of two milky eyes swivelled in his direction, vague

---

* There were revivals of Handel's oratorio *Samson* (1741) at the Theatre Royal, Covent Garden in 1753, 1754, and 1755.

and unseeing beneath a large and trembling wig, and scampered off across the piazza.

Most of his excursions were spent skimming through a world of buckles and ankles, but it took only a scrabble up a tree, his claws sharpening nicely on the rough wood of the bark, or a scramble across a roof, rusted tiles loosening beneath his weight, for his domain to widen, his purview stretch. Scudding clouds of white and grey wigs floated beneath him, and a flow of tri-cornered hats and the canvas tops of carriages pulsed through the tangled arteries of the London streets. But cats are near-sighted. Beyond the realm of his vision was London's usual uproar, red roofs floating beneath a crowd of flags and weather vanes spinning in the smog, the stalagmites of spire, the tangle of masts along the great brown ribbon of the Thames, which froze to a shiny bronze in winter. Looming far above all was the great dome of St Paul's, its baritone boom ringing out beneath the silvery chiming that assaulted a certain pair of ginger ears, hour upon hour, from a choir of singing saints, St Peter Upon Cornhill, St Mary Le Bow, St Anne, St Giles in Cripplegate, St Margaret Lothbury, and the tenor of St Sepulchre near the Old Bailey, whose bell-ringer would strike an execution knell for the prisoners in nearby Newgate while their last hours seeped away in wide-eyed candlelit torment, and their last minutes were paraded in front of a baying crowd, which cheered at the clatter of the stool, at the creaking of the rope, at the swinging pair of dusty shoes, just brushing an inquisitive ginger nose as, on one of Jeoffry's walks through the city, he stumbled upon the reek of death.

It was the November of 1755, by which time Jeoffry, as old as the decade, had grown adept at the navigation of the London streets. He was settled once again in his regular spot opposite the Drury Lane Theatre. For nearly an hour he had been watching a steady and mysterious stream of people go inside. A babel of unknown languages shot its way across the street and into his ears, and his claws flexed with longing as he saw, being carried into the theatre, lustrous reels of brightly coloured silks, handfuls of beads, headdresses and swords and, at one astonishing moment, as the light began to dim on that cold wintry afternoon, a procession of lustrous yellow globes bobbing their way into the building, held aloft on sticks, as if the stars of the sky had fallen to earth and were floating along the chilly street. They were Chinese lanterns, lit from within by candles – but little did Jeoffry know that the theatre was hosting a spectacular ballet called *Les Fêtes Chinoises*. When a dragon arrived, its garishly painted visage all but hiding the men who were carrying it along the road and into the theatre, he considered turning tail and fleeing, but held his ground.

Thirty minutes later the cold threatened to become intolerable, and Jeoffry was just about to return home, when a carriage drew up that he knew, somehow, as cats can know things they should not, was different from the other vehicles that thundered their way in and out of his life. Crowds were gathered, shouting, cheering. The coachmen seemed dressed with especial extravagance. A trumpeter heralded the opening of the door; a river of green (or so Jeoffry perceived it) suddenly splashed from the door of the carriage, which opened (Jeoffry prowled closer) to reveal a grand boot, a buckle of astonishing glitter, a white-stockinged leg into which a garter of gold thread appeared to slice painfully. Jeoffry had slunk close enough now to put a tentative paw out onto the green river, to look up into a blue waistcoat of impossible luxury, and beyond it, rolls of neck. The face, all but hidden by the brocaded stomach beneath it, peered mistily down, and looked at Jeoffry. Jeoffry looked up into the face. The face went on its way, but had smiled, briefly. For a cat may look at a king.

The moment led Jeoffry to linger, although he quickly had to scamper out of the way of further

carriages that queued up along the road, the dung
steaming in the cold gutters beneath the flame of
the street lamps, the night quite dark now. A flut-
ter of frock coats disappeared into the theatre, and
Jeoffry, who lived in the moment, thought little
more about them, distracted by the speeding bullet
of a mouse that shot ill-advisedly out of a hole in
the bottom of a nearby building, and was speed-
ily despatched by the swipe of a well-practised
paw. (He had become an efficient mouser, cheer-
ily crunching his way through his catch before
tenderly depositing the gallbladder at the foot of
Nancy's bed in gratitude for her kindness.) Then
he heard a great roar from within, which did not
sound to him like a familiar roar (of, say, laugh-
ter or applause). Suddenly, there was a scream, a
great crash, as of broken glass, and then another
crash; suddenly, there were men in the street,
shouting, shouting. Women were being hauled
out of the theatre in bundles of skirts and smelling
salts, and Jeoffry saw a man in a long coat swipe at

another with his long sword, and only just avoided being hit by a quick spray of blood that spattered the road.

He knew nothing of riots, of the conflict with France that had made the English audiences unhappy at seeing the French dancers perform in the *Fêtes Chinoises*. He cared little for the class divide that had led the aristocratic gentlemen to leave the comfort of their boxes so as violently to subdue the patriotic shouts of the rabble in the cheaper seats below.[2] Jeoffry fled, and barely left the bordello for a whole week, preferring to hide under Nancy's bed or pad nervously into the courtyard. He was sensible: the riots lasted for five days, and the theatre scenery was broken beyond repair. Chandeliers fell; it rained glass. And when Jeoffry did venture back out, in that winter of 1755, he never again found that green-gloved hand that had stroked him each afternoon outside the theatre off Drury Lane. He preferred to pick his way along the mouse-rich cobbles closer to home, in the

black hat lay neatly placed on top of his boots in another corner of the candlelit room, and Jeoffry was pondering killing it. It took all three of them a while to realise that a sudden clamour of shouts and slams – oh, horrible repeat for the cat of nightmares past – was not outside the house but within it. At one particularly loud bang, perhaps a piece of furniture being overturned, the army officer sprang from the bed and flattened himself on the carpet as if by reflex. For a split second the army officer looked directly at Jeoffry, whose eyes flashed from the gloom. For a split second Jeoffry looked at the army officer. Nancy, a quick thinker, had heard a scream from the floor below and the unsuitably farcical noise of doors opening and shutting with unusual speed and urgency. She hauled the officer to his feet, shouted something that Jeoffry did not understand, and the man fled the room, uselessly preserving his modesty with a hastily grabbed epaulette. Women were running along the corridor and up and down the stairs, and more furniture seemed to be being overturned. Jeoffry could single out a particularly loud bellow that was less shrill than the rest. It was Mother Douglas, roaring words that her girls had not known she knew. Jeoffry thought it wise to stay put; Nancy almost certainly thought otherwise, but had no choice. Within moments a black-coated constable holding a truncheon and a lantern (recently extinguished, Jeoffry could smell) had barged his way into the room, leaving (so Jeoffry noted with hypocritical disapproval) a smear of mud on the carpet. The constable was shouting louder than was necessary, and pushed over a chair, equally unnecessarily. Nancy shouted to match him, but struggle was useless, so she didn't bother, and, naked underneath the army officer's coat, which was twisted so that the brass buttons pushed a blotch of red welts into her skin, she was marched speedily out of the room. Jeoffry's last glimpse of her was of a pair of blistered heels, the sprinkle of fleabites that she had scratched into infection, vowing to turn the cat out of the house, one of these days. He did not know where she was going, and he would not see her again. The door was slammed.

It was not just Mother Douglas's establishment that had buckled to the raids; the authorities had worked their way along the bordellos of Covent Garden.[3] But Mother Douglas was an especially good catch, and she spent the night locked in a local prison, before a well-wisher paid her bail and she was released. A girl within her whorehouse had tattled, hence the raids, and entries from Nancy's diary seem very clearly to reveal the culprit. "A very interesting conversation with a Mr S— W—," she writes (Saunders Welch was the High Constable of Holborn), "who, after a long period in which he evidently felt I was of little consequence, finally listened with open ears to some interesting facts about the true nature of the various establishments at CG, and the dealings of Mrs D—." Seemingly a client had offered her a regular position elsewhere, in exchange for similar services. Mother Douglas had once too often lost her temper, which was already heavily frayed by pain and alcohol, her legs mottled and ballooning with dropsy.

Nancy's information seems to have bought her release, and at some point in the late summer of 1758 she was free briefly to return to the house, which passed into different ownership the following year, to collect her things. When she re-entered the sanctuary of her room, which was musty and cold, even on that summer morning, she was distracted by the puddles of wax that the abandoned candles had left over mantelpiece and windowsill, and did not think immediately to look under the bed. When she did, she saw that the cat wasn't there. She asked after him, as her fellow ladies returned to the house, and got quite cross with Mrs Craft when she professed herself too harried and upset to be bothering about flea-ridden cats. She kept half an eye out for a flash of ginger at ankle height when picking her way through the colonnades and muck of the piazza, ignoring the jeers of locals who had witnessed the raid. And soon, it seems, she forgot him. A few years later, in 1761, she appeared in Mr Harris's list of Covent Garden Ladies, the annual directory of prostitutes then at work in Georgian London, having found her way to a house in the archway known as the "Devil's Gap", near Drury Lane:

> Nancy Burroughs: Very impudent and very ugly; chiefly a dealer with old fellows. It is reported that she uses more birch rods in a week than Westminster School in a twelve-month. In a word, this lady will condescend to oblige her companion in whatsoever way he likes, if she is but sure of being well paid for it.[4]

But Jeoffry is never mentioned again in her ever-briefer diary entries, which soon give out altogether.

So what of Jeoffry? He had crouched under the bed, aquiver at the noise and the unexpected disruption, for nearly an hour, watching the candles burn down, and not feeling that his hunger had yet become intense enough to risk a padding prowl along the corridor and down the back staircase that led to the kitchens and the outside world. His nerves were alert, so much so that when the door suddenly opened he yowled in alarm. It was a pair of black boots, different to the ones that had come before, but equally terrifying. Hugh Collins was only fourteen, only a volunteer, as most constables were. He had not told his parents the true purpose of the raid he had signed up to, merely said that he wanted to help out the Bow Street Runners, and he had liked the idea of holding a truncheon and wearing a black hat. His older cousin had told him that, if he helped with the Covent Garden raids, he might see some of the ladies without their clothes on. This had proved true, though while he had stared gaping at the steady stream of naked or half-naked men that poured out into the piazza and melted into the darkness, he had been too nervous in the presence of the women to do anything but avert his eyes. Once the ladies had been carted off to Bridewell, the City Marshal had instructed Hugh to make a final inspection of the upper rooms, to check for anyone in hiding. In Nancy's room he helped himself to fistfuls of jewellery that he did not realise was costume, goggled at the powders and paints on her dressing table, and felt strangely stirred by the display of stockings and undergarments, still lying where the army officer had thrown them.

When Jeoffry yowled, Hugh Collins spun round, half expecting to find another "person of ill repute", as the High Constable had called them, and wondering if he could face the confrontation. But his brain, backward as it was often said to be, told him he had heard a cat, and he began to search for it. Soon he was on his hands and knees, looking under the bed at Jeoffry. The cat hissed at him violently, but something in Hugh realised that he could not leave a living animal in an all-but-deserted house. Jeoffry was lying on clothing of some kind, and was

pulled out quite easily when Hugh tugged at the
nearest embroidered sleeve. Jeoffry did not always
run or scrabble when he was cornered; often he
froze, his limbs first tight and then floppy with
panic. Hugh Collins's wrists escaped their flaying,
on this occasion, though not on others. He had
been given a canvas bag in which he was supposed
to place any confiscated bracelets or necklaces that
the girls were still wearing. He put Jeoffry in the
bag and, unthinking, tied the handles together,
before realising that wasn't sensible and unty-
ing them again. Dithering, he suddenly grabbed
at the blue dress Jeoffry had been lying on, and
stuffed it, scrunched, into the bag, as a peace offer-
ing. The cat, purring in alarm, as cats can, curled
round and round in the bag, which made it both
tricky and heavy to carry. When asked by a senior
constable of the watch what he had got in the bag,
Hugh, instead of turning out the animal into the
street as he had intended, muttered and went red
and clutched the canvas to his chest. The senior

constable, suspecting some minor theft, of jewellery or a watch or, most likely, a pair of silk drawers saved for some fumbled private entertainment later on, chuckled at the boy and walked off.

It is at this point that Jeoffry drops from history for a murky twelve months. He appears to have spent them with Hugh Collins, although it is unknown where, and in what conditions. Likely poor ones, and it is a proof of the boy's clumsy love for the cat, and perhaps the cat's for him, that Jeoffry was still with him after the space of a year in which he could happily have set off for a life on the streets. Testimonies written not long afterwards describe a healthy cat in the prime of life, rather than one of mangy fur and visible bones. Just one possible report of their time together has been discovered, in the form of a brief article published in the *Gazetteer and London Daily Advertiser*, on 1 November 1758:

On Wednesday last a large Crowd gathered
on Flitcroft–street by the Church of St Giles
in the Fields; it is reported that a young Man,
some sixteen years old, and with a noticeable
scarring across his Face, was seen climbing
up the Wall of the Church and onto the First
Ledge of the Great Spire, where he stood in
an attempt to fetch a Cat who was meshed
in the Branches of a Tree on Flitcroft–street;
an Audience gathered, some of whom
endeavoured to persuade him to descend by
spreading Coats upon the Ground, while
others expressed the Opinion that the only just
Punishment for his Blasphemy and Trespass
was to suffer some grave Accident; still others
were certain that there was no Cat to be seen
in the Tree, although afterwards there were
Reports of the Animal's safe Return to *Terra-
Firma*, and of the Boy's receiving a public
Scolding from the Rev. Francklyn.

No further news of the incident appears to survive, and while it is impossible to confirm that the article refers to Hugh Collins's efforts to retrieve Jeoffry from the top branches of a tree (perhaps refusing, rather than unable, to come down), the synchronicities are striking. They are also troublesome, in their implication that Hugh was living in the overpopulated district of St Giles, at the southern tip of Camden, which contained London's most notorious and insanitary slum.

Perhaps it was for this reason that, in the clammy August of 1759, a year after the raid, Hugh Collins decided to give up the travails of London life. Evidence of his fondness for Jeoffry is further revealed by the fact that, instead of forgetting the cat or turning him out of doors, he laid plans for his future. Something at the back of Hugh's mind had remembered an aunt of his, or someone he was told to call aunt, a tough, ruddy woman with a moustache that frightened him almost as much as the fact that she worked in the madhouse, saying that she was after a dog, or else a cat, to calm the newest and most disturbed of her lunatics.

Hugh had few belongings to pack. He wrenched himself free from his parents' protestations, and carried Jeoffry with some trepidation to the asylum, the cat's fur irritating the eczema that erupted across the boy's chest at times of stress or excitement. They arrived at the back door of the building, close to the brown flow of the river, and were greeted by a clucking but not unkind middle-aged woman in a rough white apron and with even rougher hands, which held the cat firmly around the middle. Jeoffry had long since given up the fight and hung limp and bored in her clutch, with only a vague eye on escape. He knew himself to be far enough away from all that was warm and familiar that flight would lead nowhere safe; nor had he received treatment to make him feel escape was necessary. Time enough for that, though flight seemed a little more appealing as the asylum nurse squished him awkwardly beneath her arm so as to give her nephew a currant bun with one hand and a smack with the other. And by the time Jeoffry was being conveyed along corridors, through a world of wails and cries that slashed at his ears like heavy rope, his legs began to scrabble against the stained cambric of Dorcas Ackerley's apron. Soon she had him into the room she was looking for, deposited him onto the grubby wooden floorboards, said a few words to the man who was sitting on a chair by the window, and then went away in a brisk jangle of keys.

His charge handed over, Hugh hurried to a carriage that, his cousin had promised, would take him to a coast where a sailor acquaintance could help him stow away. Somehow he got himself into the airless belly of HMS *Essex*, which, four months later, in the cold November of 1759, the third of the seven years that the great powers of Europe spent at war with one other, foundered in a maze of rocks and reefs while chasing a French ship in the aftermath of the Battle of Quiberon Bay.

Hugh was struck by a falling mast as the ship lumbered onto its side, a grey porridge spilling from his head across the sloping quarterdeck, and the local women found nothing worth stealing from the swollen wreck of his body when the sea finally threw him up onto the rocks of a foreign shore.

And Jeoffry sat in a room with the poet called Christopher Smart.

3

THE POET

1759

On his first day in the asylum Jeoffry, now nine years old and approaching middle age, took refuge under a simple wooden bedframe. Over the next three hours he stared suspiciously out at a small, plain room with whitewashed walls, and a chair in which, evidently, a man was sitting, in stillness and in silence. Christopher Smart did not try to coax Jeoffry out of the bed, which of course meant that Jeoffry ventured out all the quicker to discover the portly, slightly swollen, completely bald man sitting so still and silent in the chair, smelling of sweat and tobacco. The cat found that to look into the small dark eyes was to fall into the scummy black water of a deep well, mildewed with sadness and weariness, while on the play of its surface there flickered a wild and wayward intelligence. In future years he would not tire of the depths of experience they contained, nor their habit of shifting from shiny radiance to a matt vacancy, tarnishing with a shift of the cloud.

Underneath the eyes were a small sharp nose, thin lips, a chin rolling into a stubbled neck, and cobwebs of veins spun in the creases and pouches of this fascinating face. Smart, very slowly, held his sausage fingers out in front of him. Ink had crusted under his ridged nails and dried in blotches on his skin. Jeoffry, very slowly, and after a full minute's appraisal, pushed his nose, quite forcefully, into the outstretched hand, which balled itself into a fist the exact size of his head, and for some seconds the man's fist and the cat's head pushed into each other. Tremors shot through Jeoffry's tail, which stood upright, shivering as if in a gust of cold wind. And from then on they were friends.

Or maybe it didn't happen like that at all. Jeoffry's history is a murky one, and some imagination has to come into play. More certain, though not quite, is the history of Christopher Smart. Jeoffry will forgive his biographer for putting the starring role to one side, just for a page or two, while a major supporting player is briefly introduced.

A delicate and frail baby, Christopher Smart was born in Kent in 1722, while Jeoffry's great-grandparents roamed the earth. Later, Smart would proclaim his ancestry as aristocratic with a frequency that implies it was not quite aristocratic enough. Although he was born on a grand estate, his father, Peter, was not its owner but its steward. Christopher was a grammar-school boy, working diligently at his Latin and his Greek, but the bosky Kentish childhood was interrupted by his father's sudden death. Eleven-year-old Christopher found himself living in a world of grief and debt. His mother, Winifred, took Christopher and his two sisters, both older than him, to live with relatives in Durham. He went up to Cambridge in 1739, becoming a "sizar" at Pembroke College, his studies funded on condition that he undertake various menial jobs such as waiting on the Fellows' table.

He wandered through the college's small court-yard, either deep in the cracked bindings and thick pages of some ancient verses, or gazing up at the college's chapel, symmetrical and perfect, the first design ever to be commissioned from the great Christopher Wren. Soon he was awarded a scholarship; by 1743 he was a Fellow; that same year he published a Latin translation of Alexander Pope's "Ode on St Cecilia's Day". A life beckoned of scholarship and tobacco, poetry and debt. Likewise alluring were bachelorhood and bordellos, until, late in the decade, he fell in love first with a young lady named Harriot Pratt, who seems not to have reciprocated his affection, and second with a "lass with the golden locks" named Anna Maria Carnan, who did, and whom he married in 1752.

Christopher Smart's elder daughter, Marianne, was born in May 1753; his younger, Elizabeth, arrived the following year. Family life necessitated a move from Cambridge to London, and he took lodgings near to St James's Park, soon familiarising

himself with Grub Street, that long road of build-
ings in Moorfields, romantically seedy, that housed
a seemingly infinite number of writers, would-be
writers, failed writers, all crammed in together
with the publishers and booksellers on whom their
livelihoods depended, all arguing and quarrelling
and making up again in the area's coffee houses,
and availing themselves of the brothels that were
rather cheaper than the establishment in which
Jeoffry was at that moment being raised. Smart
wrote verses and articles for anyone who would
publish him – some sacred, some profane; some
English, some Latin; some original, some trans-
lated. Among his *noms de plume* were Mrs Mary
Midnight and Ebenezer Pentweazle. He expe-
rienced the requisite number of literary feuds, in
print and in person, that befits any struggling
writer attempting to make his way in the world.
He befriended figures such as Dr Johnson (corpu-
lent and gouty); Henry Fielding (likewise); Tobias
Smollett (rather thinner, long-nosed, acidic); and

was settling onto the fringes of eighteenth-century literary life and moving slowly inward, his works showing that typical combination of conveyor-belt churn-out and genuine inspiration that distinguishes his era's astonishingly productive men of letters. Typical too was the way his earnings did not satisfy the expense of his family or his taste for extravagance.

They moved to Islington, Smart began work on editing a weekly paper, and in 1755 he suffered a fit. Overwork? Exhaustion? Epilepsy? Who knows, but he had a seizure, and Dr Johnson himself made a financial contribution to keep him afloat. Smart recovered. And he thanked God for it. His poetry, thenceforth a skilful combination of seriousness, parody, even erotica, took a shift to the devout. "Rejoice always," exhorts St Paul in his first letter to the Thessalonians, "pray without ceasing, give thanks in all circumstances." Smart did. He began to pray, and he did not stop, and a commission of lunacy was taken out against him.

The cause of the commission has been meat for scholarly argument ever since. Perhaps his publisher (John Newbery, his wife's stepfather) lost his temper after years of mutual dislike and unpaid debts. Perhaps Smart suffered from what doctors might today call bipolar disorder, his depression exacerbated by financial worry, by alcohol, even by syphilis. "I have," he wrote, "a greater compass of mirth and melancholy than another." His new-found zealotry combined with an episode of mania that drew public attention. In the poem he came to write, in which Jeoffry was to play so important a role, Smart admitted:

> For I blessed God in St. James's Park till
> I routed all the company.
> For the officers of the peace are at variance
> with me and the watchman smites me with
> his staff.

Let us picture him as the shadows lengthen over the flower beds in St James's Park, his incessant and disturbing prayer echoing out across the canal, startling the pelicans on the water and the canoodling couples in the trees, drowning the distant thunder of carriages as they drive past Buckingham House, and alerting a park warder, who strikes the raving poet with his staff. Word reached Dr Johnson:

> My poor friend Smart shewed the disturbance of his mind, by falling upon his knees, and saying his prayers in the street, or in any other unusual place. Now although rationally speaking, it is greater madness not to pray at all, than to pray as Smart did, I am afraid there are so many who do not pray that their understanding is not called in question.[5]

Smart seems first to have been incarcerated, likely in a private asylum, in 1756, as Jeoffry scurried around the Covent Garden streets. On 6 May

1757 he was admitted to St Luke's Hospital for Lunatics on Old Street, his name optimistically entered in the ledgers with the description "curable patient". He spent a year and a week at St Luke's, and on 12 May 1758 was discharged, "uncured", a month before Jeoffry was rescued from the silent ruins of Mother Douglas's bordello. Swimming through fatigue but restored to his wits, assuming he ever lost them, he then spent time recuperating either with family, or in yet another private asylum. He appeared again in society early the following year, when in February 1759 the great actor-manager David Garrick, whom Jeoffry had known well, acted in a double bill "for the Benefit of a Gentleman, well known in the Literary World, who is at present under very unhappy Circumstances".[6] A brief return to lodgings in St James's did not end well. By late August he was confined once again in an asylum. Dorcas Ackerley, watching helplessly as the poet combined great stretches of mournful silence with incessant and hysterical shouting, refusing to touch the steaming bowl of oatmeal she had brought him, thought vaguely that what he needed was an animal of some kind, for company.

Smart's biographers have not settled on the location of the asylum in which he, and consequently Jeoffry, were incarcerated. Was it the private house of a Mr Potter at Bethnal Green, where his daughter later remembered being taken for a melancholy visit? Or was it the private house of Mr Turlington at Chelsea? Perhaps it was both. The great music historian Charles Burney, recently returned to London after a period at Norfolk recovering from a lung complaint, told his friend Dr Johnson that he was vexed "to hear of poor Kit's going to Chelsey", and Dr Johnson replied, "but a madman must be confined, sir, at Chelsey or elsewhere."[7]

It was a period of enlightenment when it came to the private care of the mentally disturbed, whether at Chelsea or Bethnal Green. The private institution to which Jeoffry had been carried did not fit the standard conception of a Hogarthian eighteenth-century madhouse, with crowds of passers-by jeering through spyholes at naked lunatics sprawling and yelling amid filth and dysentery. Jeoffry found himself in a room that did not smell of kindness, but nor did it smell of cruelty. Further scents carried on dusty sunbeams through an open door promised at least a scrap of the outside world, to be explored by cat and poet alike. Nevertheless, as he snuffled his way around the grubby skirting boards and sought out the best hiding places, Jeoffry discovered the iron rings at the four corners of the simple bedstead, startlingly cold to the touch, even on this muggy summer's day, and he scratched tentatively at the pungent leather straps that were threaded through them. The Madhouse Act of 1774, which set out a legal framework for the regulation of insane asylums, would come too late for Jeoffry and Christopher Smart.[8] Yet Smart sat for now unchained, and the greatest indication of the kindness of the regime was exhibited first in the toleration of the cat (nobody would make a move to take Jeoffry away from Smart over the years of their incarceration), and second in the large sheets of paper that lay on the small wooden table by the window next to Smart's wig stand, two or three jars of ink, a pile of white quill pens, and a small rosewood pounce pot full of a fine powder that he would sprinkle across the page to dry his glistening script, as if seasoning food.

Smart had begun to write his masterpiece earlier that year. Not for some weeks would Jeoffry become confident enough to leap up and onto the table, but soon he would scatter pawfuls of muddy prints across a pile of papers, each covered in Smart's elegant tiny italics, the handwriting bearing very few signs of anything resembling mental disturbance: there are few corrections or blots or wayward curlicues. The long tendrils of verse, eighty to a page, lay ordered and level in their serried ranks of devotion. The poem's title was an instruction, an imperative: *Jubilate Agno* (*Rejoice in the Lamb*). And the poem itself is obedient to its own title, being a long hymn of praise to Smart's God, gathering up in its capacious embrace the wonders of the natural world, and extolling them to worship the Lord. Could Jeoffry have read, he would have made out the opening sentences:

> Rejoice in God, O ye Tongues; give the glory
>   to the Lord, and the Lamb.
> Nations, and languages, and every Creature,
>   in which is the breath of Life.
> Let man and beast appear before him, and
>   magnify his name together.

And so they do. Jeoffry settled himself onto the cool comfort of the paper and curled up amid many hundreds of lines in which Biblical figures are combined with animals of every kind in order to praise the Lord: "Let Abraham present a Ram" … "Let Nimrod, the mighty hunter, bind a Leopard to the altar" … "Let Gideon bless with the Panther" … "Let Job bless with the Worm" … and so on. Like most visions, it hovers on the border between the absurd and the sublime; it is hard to tell whether the poem is in a state of ecstasy or banging its head against the wall. In a second section Smart continued the pattern – "Let Elizur rejoice with the Partridge" ... "Let Helon rejoice with the Woodpecker" – but introduced an answering line, each beginning with the word "For", in which his own life began to intrude. The two sides of the poem start to sing antiphonally, like two choirs calling and responding to one another across the nave of St Paul's:

Let Elizur rejoice with the Partridge, who is a
    prisoner of state and is proud of his keepers.
For I am not without authority in my jeopardy,
    which I derive inevitably from the glory of
    the name of the Lord. [...]

Let Peter rejoice with the moon fish who
    keeps up the life in the waters by night.

For I pray the Lord JESUS that cured the
    LUNATICK to be merciful to all my breth-
    ren and sisters in these houses.

And, leaping noisily out at Jeoffry's biographer:

Let Shephatiah rejoice with the little Owl,
    which is the wingged Cat.
For I am possessed of a cat, surpassing in
    beauty, from whom I take occasion to bless
    Almighty God.

At certain moments the "Let" sections of the poem
give out, leaving only the "For", and eventually, in
the summer of 1760, Smart would devote many of
them to the long and oft-anthologised description of
his cat, entranced and entrancing, that prefaces this
biography: "For I will consider my Cat Jeoffry …"
Anthologising and excerpting can play strange tricks
on the reader, carving lines from a larger whole, and
implying importance where none was intended.

Examining the manuscript of *Jubilate Agno*, of which only fragments survive, it is quite a shock to see Jeoffry's portrait creep up on the reader, beginning mid-page, with no pause or fanfare, after a sequence of extended wordplay on the word "bull". It should be remembered too that the lines about Jeoffry ("For … For … For …") were presumably linked with an additional sequence ("Let … Let … Let …"), now lost, and that this most famous of all poems may in reality be only one side of an intricate ribcage of verse.[*] The section about Jeoffry ends with a shrug – "For he can creep" – that appears at the very bottom of a page whose immediate successors are now lost; Smart may have written more about his cat than we know.

Speedily *Jubilate Agno* had made clear what Smart thought of cats: "Let Anna bless God with the Cat, who is worthy to be presented before the throne of grace, when he has trampled upon the idol in his prank." In the book of Baruch (not, in

---

[*]   Elena Passarello has imagined the missing half in *Animals Strike Curious Poses* (Louisville: Sarabande Books, 2017).

most Protestant forms of Christianity, considered part of the Bible) the Babylonian idols are held in contempt by "bats, swallows, and birds, and the cats also". Certainly Jeoffry, as Smart was soon to discover, was not one for either idleness or idolatry.

And so, as the cat and the poet got used to their shared existence in their four-walled world, Smart continued writing his great poem. For him the act of writing was itself a form of worship, and Jeoffry would watch him occasionally fall to his knees as he began to write. The verse (of which over 1,700 lines survive) is whimsical in its ecstasy, and ecstatic in its whimsy: a paean of praise, but also a kind of almanac, a journal of Smart's incarceration, as he added three or so lines each day. Soon political leaders of the time, along with members of Smart's estranged family, or names from the obituary lists, even the local postman, begin to parade through the lines. Insects crawl around the verbs and birds soar above adjectives. Mythical creatures jostle alongside explications and criticisms of the scientific theories of Mr Newton or Mr Locke. Gemstones are invoked in praise of the Lord. (Towering above Jeoffry on Smart's writing desk was a pile of books that kept the poet company over those many years and whose deliciously musty smell, of grass and vanilla, wriggled in the cat's nose: a King James Bible on top of a Latin thesaurus; a guide for London pharmacists written in Latin; a history of plants; and a gardener's dictionary.)

Smart's poem twists and knots the language into puns and double meanings and new meanings, as if even wordplay were an exemplar of inclusivity: all definitions, as they crowd within a single word, are welcome to praise the Lord. *Jubilate Agno* is a magnificat, a song of praise by all creation to glorify God; and it would not take long for Jeoffry to become Christopher Smart's magnifi-cat. As when in a painting the viewer suddenly glimpses an image of the artist himself reflected in a mirror, Smart suddenly heaves into view, in sad and self-aware glimpses of his solitary journey to the make sure his new companion was not in physical discomfort. Every three hours or so, Jeoffry would tentatively slink to Smart's chair, rub his head into it, and then frisk away again whenever Smart sneezed or turned over a piece of paper. It was during one of these excursions that the four close-cropped frock-coated men marched into the room. They were accompanied by a physician who held out for Smart a bottle of some thick liquid that dripped slowly into a spoon. Smart said he would not take it, and the physician said he must, and Smart again refused. And the physician said he must. What happened next lasted a minute and an eternity.

One of the four men in the coats kicked Jeoffry roughly out of the way. A booted foot caught the cat painfully in his ribs and pushed him into the wall, where he bashed his head against the plaster. He yowled in pain and fear, made to bolt, found that one of his hind legs collapsed beneath him, trembled, and froze, his ears flat. Nobody noticed him, and the sound he made had been drowned by Christopher Smart's own shouting. Without even bothering to push the poet away from his desk, and with the ease that comes of long practice, one of the men tipped Smart's chair back, and another held him fast by the ankles. The two others suddenly whipped from nowhere a set of hooks. They had four in all, about a foot long, sharply curving at the end, rusted and treacherous. Through a mist of fear and pain, Jeoffry saw the men insert the four hooks into Smart's mouth: two were over his bottom jaw, two over his top jaw, and the men then pulled. Something gurgled and boiled in Smart's throat, and the metal of the hooks scraped against his toothless gums. Through a crooked elbow, under an arm, between a pair of legs, Jeoffry caught glimpses of his companion as a tusked creature. Smart's eyes were wide and wild, his nostrils flared, and his mouth was a terrifying black hub at the centre of a wheel of spokes. Suddenly he collapsed in his chair, but the hooks, pulling his jaws wider open still, splayed from his head like a four-pronged compass or weathervane, like spears in a harpooned whale. The doctor tipped up the bottle into the open mouth, the hooks went promptly slack, Smart choked and retched, and the men left, just as Smart vomited a blood-flecked gruel down the front of his yellowing shirt. A foaming crimson thread drooled from the corner of his mouth and into the greying bristles of his neck. They had not even upset his inkwell. "Let Andrew rejoice with the Whale," Smart wrote in his poem on 1 September 1759, "who is arrayd in beauteous blue and is combination of bulk and activity." And, on the opposite page: "For they work me with their harping-irons, which is a barbarous instrument, because I am more unguarded than others."[9]

Christopher Smart and his cat Jeoffry then sat in their own worlds for some time before venturing into each other's. Jeoffry was sore, his leg sprained rather than broken, and in his animal confusion he was temporarily unable to perceive Smart his friend and the doctor's man his enemy: all humans were alike persecutors. Eventually he hobbled on three legs towards the cool dusty haven under Smart's bed, and Smart bent down to lift him, with an infinite gentleness, onto his lap. Jeoffry's claws pricked through the cotton of his breeches, but Smart sat still until, surprisingly, the cat settled, and with a quick simple movement that stopped the poet's heart, pushed his head into the face that hovered above him and licked, twice, with the hooked bristles of his rough tongue, at the blood that had trickled from the corner of Smart's mouth.

There followed three days that Jeoffry spent mainly under the bed, licking his wounds, and neither of them could touch food. Smart lifted the cat on and off the chair and the bed, and carried him outside twice a day, morning and evening. Jeoffry scratched him only once, when his leg twisted awkwardly in Smart's arms. By the end of that week the cat could get himself onto the chair or bed of his own accord, and did so, most evenings, sitting beside Smart at the desk, or curling himself into the man's back when he went to bed. The poet threw off his blankets in the summer stuffiness of the small room, but never threw off the cat. And so the light dimmed in the endless evenings, until finally it was not light at all, and they sat in the dark. Cat and man, in the small plain room, in the dark. And in the dark they fell asleep, as best they could; sleeping, side by side, in the dark.

4

THE FLOWERS

1759–1762

corners, of Smart's meaning, tracing his way into a cry, a sigh, an inflection, and he understood much. To Jeoffry, the man smelled of fear, and as the days passed in the small room, and then the weeks, and then the months, the cat grew used to periods in which Smart would sit on the chair or lie on the bed neither sleeping nor, at least as Jeoffry perceived it, especially wakeful. The man's eyes were open, and not exactly glazed so much as dulled and shallow, the gold-flecked brown from which Jeoffry could usually read much now lustreless and empty. Around Smart stretched something that was not there, but which Jeoffry could see all the same: an absence of light, like a silk blanket that was not black but blank, that was not dark but vacuous, empty of meaning, devoid of sense. Underneath it, as if the blanket were spread over a jostling crowd of birds, there were sharp and furious movements and jabs, pricking Smart all over his body, clustering around his head and at the back of his neck. On some days the blanket and its jabs sent Smart mad, and on other days it sent him still, and sometimes Jeoffry could see that it wasn't there at all. Jeoffry knew it for what it was, but what it was he could not say.

Christopher Smart praying was likewise a source of enduring terror and fascination to his cat. The poet had considered Jeoffry seemingly at worship, circling delightfully "seven times round in elegant quickness" (in inappropriately devilish advocacy, the cynical biographer must interject that cats occasionally chase their own tails, with little thought of the Lord). But Jeoffry often had the chance to consider his poet, Christopher, and would cower from a dark corner while the man fell to his knees, rocking back and forth, his whole body tense with belief. Veins would rise on the dome of his head like rivers on a globe, and a fervent muttering would change, with speedy and terrifying crescendo, into a rhythmical and repetitive shouting. Smart's hands beat at his temples, and his forehead burned with the effort, and tears spilled down his face. Often this would lead to his restraint, and on the days when a member of the asylum's staff could not calm him with a direct gaze and soothing conversation, he would be dragged to the bed and tied down, his whole body strained by the continuous thundering of his hysterical liturgy.

The two grew used to their imprisonment together, and life continued, and incarceration became normality. Smart wrote each day at his poem, and submitted more calmly to the physician's request to take his medicine; never again did the men arrive with their hooks. Smart's room had a door that creaked open onto a small garden that ran along the side of the building: a strip of long grass, crisping first in the sunshine and then in the frost, bordered with flower beds which the poet was permitted to tend with ardent devotion. Perhaps friends (he was permitted visitors) brought him seeds or bulbs. In spring, daffodils trumpeted through the window, and, at night, the darkness sang with the delicious sharpness of hyacinths. Later in the year roses bloomed and carnations opened, and Jeoffry would push his face into the frayed edges of their petals, while Smart twined sweet peas round a makeshift trellis that leant against a high wall topped with coiled wire. Jeoffry had instantly known there would be no possibility of escape. "For the doubling of flowers is the improvement of the gardners talent," Smart wrote.

> For the flowers are great blessings. [...]
> For flowers are good both for the living and
>   the dead.
> For there is a language of flowers.
> For there is a sound reasoning upon all flowers.
> For elegant phrases are nothing but flowers.
> For flowers are peculiarly the poetry of Christ.
> For flowers are medicinal.
> For flowers are musical in ocular harmony.
>   [...]
> For the blessing of God upon the grass is in
>   shades of Green visible to a nice* observer
>   as they light upon the surface of the earth.

---

*   In the sense of attentive, sharp.

Jeoffry earmarked a corner of one of the flower beds for himself, and scratched on the door each morning and evening for Smart to let him out. Dorcas Ackerley made sure to bring him a dish of whatever she could find, squeezed onto the wooden tray on which she brought in Smart's beer tankard and small portion of oatmeal. Smart would make sure to put down a bowl of water for him, and in winter smashed the ice in his ewer to get at the liquid beneath. But there are slim pickings for a cat in an asylum, and few mice made it into the tiny garden. (When he did catch them, as Smart observed, they seemed quickly to escape. The poet approves of Jeoffry's merciful attitude; the biographer wonders if an ageing hunter was losing his touch.) Jeoffry subsisted on the cheapest and most meagre of meals: fish on-the-turn, bought cheap at the market, or a glistening pile of chicken intestines pulled from a bird that was to be cooked for a doctor's meal. He would have grown thin and rangy had he somehow found a way to roam free water, chill and bright, that reflected the sunshine as he sparkled his way through the undergrowth. In the autumn, red leaves fell in a shower from a tree in the pathway behind the wall, and Jeoffry chased them. In the winter, the physicians insisted that the windows in Smart's room were kept open, and the poet and cat snuggled together in bed, or close to the small fire that made Jeoffry smell pleasingly of smoke and dust, avoiding the muddy pools of melted snow that collected under the window and left dark stains on the wooden floor. If it rained, a doctor of some kind would arrive to hustle Smart out of his clothes and outside, and through his room would tramp a parade of inmates, who did not have their own garden. They were likewise stripped naked, the young and the old, the wizened and the beautiful, the screeching and the murmuring and the silent, male and female alike. Communal washing in a downpour was a standard shortcut in asylums of the day, and Smart, executing a strange and wobbling little dance as grey rivulets of water ran down his hairless chest, seemed oddly elated, standing in the sad row of naked people scratching at their sores. A young woman's long hair whipped across her face like damp string. Some sang, some joined him in the dance or consented to be pulled to their knees in prayer. The naked crowd knelt on the patch of grass in the rain, which fell noisily into their foggy chorus of garbled and sodden worship. Others simply stood still, staring straight ahead and blinking drops from their eyelashes as the rain pooled at their feet and churned the ground into mud.[10] "For to worship naked in the Rain", Smart wrote in his poem, "is the bravest thing for the refreshing and purifying [of] the body."

The cat spent many an evening of those first months calling in despair for his previous lives, for Nancy, for Hugh Collins, for the ecstatic freedom of the London streets. He was safe, he was (mainly) warm, and he was loved, even by some of the staff. One maid in particular set great store by a nuzzle from Jeoffry when she came every other day to drag a filthy mop over the filthy floor. But for a nine-year-old cat so recently enjoying his *Wanderjahre*, incarceration took some time to get used to. And Smart would sit by the fire, the darkness crowding round his head as visible to Jeoffry as ever, thinking of his family, of his estranged wife, of his beloved daughters, packed off to some foreign convent. Together, cat and lunatic, they howled their despair to the indifferent moon.

It was a hot summer the following year, and the asylum baked, its sweating inmates displayed behind its scalding windowpanes like specimens under glass. The old king died, bellowing in agony on his chamber pot, and his grandson ascended to the throne. Christopher Smart and his cat Jeoffry knew little of this, as 1760 morphed into 1761, and little bar the weather and the progress of the flowers marked for them any difference in the weeks and months. The manuscript of *Jubilate Agno*, as far as the precise dating will allow, has a gap within it of more than a year, its first three fragments having been completed by May 1761, and the fourth, which has "Let" verses only, not taken up again until July 1762, by which time the poem has dwindled into a form of worshipping by numbers, counting the days, using names taken from the newspapers that caused editorial headaches centuries later.

Smart had his cat, his garden, and his solitude, the interruptions to which took on vast importance. He taught Latin to the children of one of his more sympathetic keepers, who paraded unwillingly into the frightening room and took some while to realise that the poet could at least talk to them with kindness, and explain ablative absolutes with easeful clarity. They enjoyed any distraction his sweet ginger cat might cause, as he tumbled across the table or curled up on their laps and prickled them with his claws.

For Jeoffry was a sociable creature, and an eleven-year-old cat should have been enjoying his prime rather than throwing himself at the four walls of a small room, or clambering up onto furniture and batting at butterflies in the garden. Perhaps we realise we are in our prime only when we are denied our chance to enjoy it. At one particularly enticing rustle from beneath a geranium, Jeoffry launched himself without thinking at what he took to be a mouse, and staggered sharply backwards with a yowl of pain as the rat sank his fangs into Jeoffry's neck and disappeared into a hole at the bottom of the brick wall. Jeoffry kept absolutely still for five seconds, before frantically attempting to lick at the pain in his neck, but, cross-eyed in his endeavour, he found it hard to reach. He had a white bib of fur around his neck like a kerchief, and white hair soon fell in a shower from the rat bite, which was deep, and gaped red and sore from his neck like a pendant. Jeoffry loped sadly inside and jumped up onto Smart's lap. Smart instantly comfort lay in tatters about him, Smart could see that a neat scab was healing over the wound, and a down of white hair was just starting to appear again around it, of impossibly velvet softness.

The horror of Jeoffry's injury aside, few ripples broke on the stagnant waters of their confinement. Smart's visitors were few, but Jeoffry made occasional contact with a number of distinguished legs: the bulging calves and hobbling feet of Dr Johnson, who dangled an enormous hand over the side of his chair to stroke Jeoffry's head, before Smart pulled him down onto his knees in order to pray ("God be gracious to Samuel Johnson" was soon added to *Jubilate Agno*) and two of the asylum's porters had to be called in to help the learned doctor back up again. More strapping were the legs of Charles Burney, who sang to Christopher Smart, and Smart cried. Jeoffry gazed curiously up at the domed forehead of Oliver Goldsmith, who talked with Smart by candlelight in the autumn evenings, reading aloud from the manuscript of a novel he had finished that year about a vicar, which he hoped would one day be published. Goldsmith did all the characters in different voices, and the two laughed together. There was something vaguely familiar about the great resonant voice of David Garrick, as he came to the asylum and recited the final scene of *King Lear*, playing all the parts. Smart cheered and clapped at the happy ending, as Lear regained his throne and Cordelia married Edgar, who declared that "truth and virtue shall at last succeed".*

As Jeoffry grew older he grew needier, not for exercise but for affection. His world had shrunk, and Smart dominated it like a monolith. If Smart sat down to write at the desk, up Jeoffry would climb, batting at Smart's pounce pot so that the

---

* Oliver Goldsmith's *The Vicar of Wakefield* (1761–62) was published in 1766 by Smart's father-in-law John Newbery, who was sent the manuscript by Dr Johnson. Nahum Tate's bowdlerised version of *King Lear* (1681) was so popular that it was used in every known performance of the play until 1838.

sand (made of powdered cuttlefish bone and as expensive for a writer to obtain as it was intriguing for a cat to smell) spilled across the table. Tangled loops of sandy pawprints would soon appear on the floorboards. When Smart lay down to sleep, Jeoffry would curl up onto his pillow and beneficently shed all over the grubby linen, or crawl onto Smart's chest and fall into a sleep so deep that Smart himself lay awake for hours lest he disturb the cat, who finally flopped nonchalantly off the bed of his own accord, leaving the poet's muscles frozen and knotted with cramp. During the day Smart pulled ribbons or strips of cloth across the floor for Jeoffry to chase, or bounced him the stopper from his beer tankard, games of which the human tired long before the cat. At night two paws would hammer on the door that led to the garden, and Smart would crawl blearily out of the bed, leading Jeoffry to decide that, actually, he had not wanted to go out after all. But perhaps a game …?

And so they went on, until the influenza arrived in England.

"For an Ague is a terror of the body," Smart wrote in *Jubilate Agno*, "when the blessing of God is withheld for a season." Influenza travelled over from the Americas to Europe in 1761, and reached London in the spring of 1762.[11] The virus raced through the city and through the asylum, and Christopher Smart coughed and the lunatics sweated and suppurated. The Black Death had not visited the city in nearly a century, but older residents still remembered how their parents and grandparents would tense with horror whenever they heard the trundle of a cart in the road outside, or how the blood drained from the faces of the elderly at the first glimpse of any bruise or swelling. Dorcas Ackerley sat by her fire and spoke in a hushed voice of her grandmother, who a century ago had found the tell-tale tumour in her groin and lived long enough to watch her skin blacken and split and feel her tongue bulge in her head. An elderly porter had had an uncle who as a boy dug the pits at Spitalfields, and who saw seven of his eight brothers thrown into the soil before joining them himself.

The death-carts trundled again; the gravediggers sweated and shivered in their beds and flies buzzed around the bodies rotting in the spring sunshine. The virus gave those with weak lungs pneumonia; those with weak hearts had heart attacks. From Chiswick to Greenwich the physicians mistook what they saw for cholera, and moaned to their colleagues about the dwindling audiences at public amputations. Babies were piled up in their dozens, like rabbits at the end of shooting season. Greengrocers and lords alike bled from their ears, their membranes haemorrhaged, and mucous ran into their chamber pots. The shops were boarded up, and the market stall from which Dorcas Ackerley occasionally remembered to buy a rattling handful of oysters for Jeoffry lay abandoned under canvas, its keeper sitting in frightened prayer by the feverish bedside of his wife and child.

Jeoffry and Christopher Smart waited for the influenza, as it chased the families fleeing the capital in frightened carriages, and was conveyed by the rats onto barges in the Thames and along the gutters of Covent Garden. The ladies in the shabby bordellos who had escaped infection sat in their rooms unvisited, in a stupor of gin and boredom. Soon the lunatics were aching and groaning in their cells, and the asylum tinkled with the noise of their blood as it was drained fruitlessly into porcelain bowls. Those physicians who were not infected prescribed cures with abandon, dropping leeches on sweating limbs as if decorating a cake with currants, and cupping any back within reach. The older inmates first went pale, and then went blue, and sat dead or dying in their chairs, while grey sheets floated lazily from the doorframes, soaked in vinegar that evaporated in the heat and left the asylum hovering in an acid mist. The fireplaces were stoked against infection even as the sunshine beat at the windows. Nauseous maids refused to clean the rooms and sat instead in the steamy kitchens, comparing powders and ointments they had purchased from the apothecaries, for whom business was booming. One inmate on the floor above Smart had been permitted to keep a bedraggled canary in a rusting cage, to whom he sang ditties every twilight. Forgotten amid the frightening spread of the fever, the bird drooped softly off its perch and died, like any plant quietly withering for lack of water.

Soon Christopher Smart's temperature soared and he took to his bed, unvisited, shouting and wailing in his delirium. The door to the garden remained locked, the fire roared, and Jeoffry drowned in the noxious stink of leaking wounds and soiled clothes, and the festering smog of illness and death that lay beneath the acrid burning of camphor and rosemary. Smart's body shuddered and shook. Humans cannot catch influenza from their cats; but cats can be infected by their humans. A brown crust formed at the corners of

Jeoffry's eyes, his mouth prickled with ulcers, and a thick saliva ran from his nose and mouth into his fur. All he could think of to do was to shut himself down, and he did so, curling into a tight ball under Smart's bed, forgotten by those who knew him, and near hibernation for three or four days. The poet lay above him, devout and forsaken, calling aloud to his God.

5

THE FLUTE

1763–1770

On 28 January 1763, long after the influenza had left the asylum and those left alive had recovered, Christopher Smart fell to his knees and added the following line to his poem *Jubilate Agno*: "God be gracious to John Sherratt." Mr Sherratt was a London merchant, and had once managed the Marylebone Pleasure Gardens, which Smart had often frequented in the days of his freedom. He and Sherratt had remained friends, and on 30 January, about a month before Jeoffry's thirteenth birthday, Sherratt simply walked into the asylum, and somehow (scholars have never been sure quite how) took his friend away with him. Smart wrote only two more lines of the poem, one of which was "Blessed be the name of Jesus in singularities and singular mercies." He held the pile of large loose sheets under one arm, and in the other a basket in which Jeoffry had spittingly resigned to be carried, his twitching nose pressing its inquisitive way between the leather straps that loosely held together the two flaps of the lid. So off they all went to John Sherratt's house, and soon afterwards Christopher Smart and his cat Jeoffry were established in rooms in St James's Park, lodging with a Mrs Barwell in her house on its south edge.

Freedom for Jeoffry, after years of incarceration, was a strange world, as oppressive in its way as imprisonment. Smart's rooms had a terrace that overlooked the park, and the building itself had a door that opened directly into it. And Jeoffry was free again, free to roam through London, to do battle with its crowds and smells, and with the dangers and trappings of urban life which, through these years in the asylum, he had almost forgotten. The world was all before him, gaping open in all its infinity and half-remembered possibility. The streets greeted him with the awkwardness of an old friend with whom one has long since fallen out of touch. At first he ventured only along Birdcage Walk and into the secret quiet of dark alleys. But soon he regained his former ways, and traced a half-mile circuit through the tangle of Westminster streets to the south of St James's Park, along York Street (now Petty France) and into Palmer and Caxton Streets, making sure always to return to Mrs Barwell's house before the door was shut. On more energetic days, he curled round the park through the Horse Guards Road, and reached, almost by accident, the great thoroughfare of the Strand, and although the width and size of the street was daunting, he had picked up speedily his street wisdom, knowing which scuffles to avoid, wistfully recognising the calls of women from doorways. He sat in the streets like any normal cat, nursing proudly within himself the secret of his incarceration, the indistinct memories of his numerous existences, as the crowds flowed around him. What especial sadness or trauma, as bespoke and individual as happiness is uniform, did each unknowable person hold in their hearts? Children came up to him, to stroke his face or pull at his tail. What would be their grief? How soon would they come to know it, and chart their unique compass of mirth and melancholy?

On one occasion he walked further up the Strand than he had meant to, chasing some shadow or other, and had the sudden horrid awareness that he was too far from home. He turned to go, but something stopped him, hovering in the corner of his eye. He had been travelling along the Strand from west to east; and meanwhile another cat had been travelling along it from east to west, and the two had met in the middle. The cat was black all over, and there was some pride and intelligence in his panther tread that made Jeoffry consider him for longer than he would any other four-legged creature met in passing on the London streets. Bravely, he scampered up to the black cat, and the two of them stood on their eight legs, appraising each other for a long and strangely charged moment. Their faces were very close, their noses twitching with inquisition. Jeoffry dared to lick the other cat in the middle of his forehead, and the other cat returned the compliment. Then they went on their way.

Jeoffry faced a tired trudge back to Mrs Barwell's. The black cat turned round and walked for some way eastwards along the Strand and finally made his way (he too had walked longer than he had intended) to a house in a small courtyard near Fleet Street, and up its main staircase into a parlour where three men were drinking coffee. The cat scratched at the sun-bleached Persian rug that covered the whitewashed floorboards, and then nudged his head into the most familiar hand in the room, which responded with a gentle twitch. Charles Burney sat rather nervously opposite Dr Johnson, watching the great scarred face melt into the upholstery of the high-backed sofa and feeling small under the appraisal of its one seeing eye. Mr Boswell was in his usual seat in the corner and saw the black cat jump up onto Dr Johnson's chest. Johnson rubbed his heavy hand along the cat's spine, whistling through his teeth, and very gently pulled at his tail, to the cat's infinite delight. "A fine cat," commented Boswell bravely, his accent

Scottish and his eyes kind – but he was trying not to sneeze at the appearance of the dusty animal, and shuffled his chair closer to the window. "Why yes, Sir," said Johnson, ignoring Boswell's discomfort and appearing to speak more to the cat than to his biographer. "But I have had cats whom I liked better than this." And then, as if concerned that the sable bundle snoozing on his capacious lap would somehow be offended, he added, "but Hodge is a very fine cat. A very fine cat indeed."

Charles Burney, feeling himself to be a spare part and wanting to fill the silence that ensued, leant over to shout into the writer's one hearing ear. "How does poor Smart do, Sir, is he likely to recover?" He had to repeat the question three times. "It seems as if his mind has ceased to struggle with the disease," Johnson eventually replied, "for he grows fat upon it." Burney attempted a joke that he knew to be feeble: "Perhaps, sir, that may be from want of exercise!" Johnson took him seriously: "No, Sir, he has partly as much exercise as he used to have, for he digs in the garden. Indeed" – and now he was starting to chuckle, letting forth a whole volley of clucks and spasms that sabotaged his speech and sent Hodge flying – "before his confinement, he used for exercise to walk to the alehouse – but he was *carried* back again." Burney made sure to laugh, and gently took the doctor's coffee cup off the arm of the sofa and out of harm's way. But suddenly Johnson was reflective. "I did not think he ought to be shut up. His infirmities were not noxious to society. He insisted on people praying with him, and I'd as lief pray with Kit Smart as anyone else." In the pause, Burney decided it was the moment to stand, as if in readiness to leave, and Boswell joined him. "Another charge," Johnson added suddenly, as he too hauled himself unsteadily to his feet, "was that he did not love clean linen. And I have no passion for it."[12] And that, Burney thought, as he stood closer to Dr Johnson to bid him goodbye and tried to stop his eyes watering, was undoubtedly true.

It is as difficult to say that Christopher Smart had recovered his sanity as it is to be certain he had ever lost it. He lived a meagre, functioning, independent existence in his new home, completing his poem *A Song to David*, which focused on the life of King David and was begun in the asylum. *Jubilate Agno* lay in a drawer somewhere, seemingly abandoned or forgotten, and almost certainly unpublishable. *A Song to David*, though, was issued in April 1763, in the first months of freedom. The critics sharpened their knives. Some thought the ecstatic verse merely further proof of its author's lunacy.

Smart's children were still in a foreign convent; his coffers were low, and his cat was thin. Money was his constant preoccupation and need. He refused to leave London, and worked every hour, blackening the walls with pipe smoke. Still Jeoffry gave him comfort in an otherwise solitary life. Still the black shadows seemed to hover around the writer's chair, even on sunlit days, as the cat watched from under the table. Still Smart prayed, or cavorted around the room shouting while flies droned on the supper that Mrs Barwell had brought in on a tray. Jeoffry took to roaming the streets for mice at nightfall, feeling it better to forage for his own food, as, often, neither Smart nor Mrs Barwell would remember to put something by for his supper.

The cat was nudging fifteen, and had begun to age, slowly and only just perceptibly. It was 1765, and the new king went mad, and talked until the foam dripped from his mouth. It was 1766, and Christopher Smart embarked upon a translation of Horace's complete verse: but a rival version appeared first, and sold well. It was 1768, and friends fell away, but in September, he was paid a visit by Charles Burney's sixteen-year-old daughter Fanny, who allowed Jeoffry to leap up onto her lap, and he lifted a tentative paw to scrape at the dangling lace of her fichu. She laughed, and stroked him into submission, surveying the room with brightly intelligent eyes. Next morning she wrote in her diary:

This ingenius [*sic*] Writer is one of the most unfortunate of men – he has been twice confined in a mad H[o]use – & but last year sent a most affecting Epistle to papa, to entreat him to lend him ½ a Guinea! – How great a pity so clever, so ingenius [*sic*] a man should be reduced to such shocking circumstances. He is extremely grave, & has still great wildness in his manner, looks & voice – 'tis impossible to see him & to think of his works, without feeling the utmost pity & concern for him.[13]

She came again the following year, remembering to bring a weaving in the shape of a mouse for Jeoffry that she had tatted herself. She was enchanted by Jeoffry, who rolled on his back the better to scrabble at the toy with his hind legs, and she recorded her dismay on hearing Smart refer to his wife,

Most looked forward to were the visits from a flautist named John Kempe, who came every other month or so to play to Smart, standing by the window while the poet sat on the faded sofa and Jeoffry scratched at its arms until he was invited up to sit with them. John Kempe played, from memory, a sonata by Handel. It was in E minor, and the flautist was hesitant, unhappy playing the solo part unaccompanied, there being no possibility of a harpsichord. There were five movements, a few minutes each, no more; and Smart called again and again to hear the Largo that bloomed at its centre. Mr Kempe grew more confident as he endlessly unspooled the ribbon of melody from his wooden instrument into the fusty air of Smart's apartment. The notes hit the panelled walls and died instantly, falling to the floor to lie at Smart's swollen feet like faded rose petals. Jeoffry was curled in Smart's lap, his eyes closing gently to the music, its pitch vaguely unpleasant to his ears, and he felt tears plash onto the scruff of his neck. Kempe later remembered that he had "often soothed the wanderings of [Smart's] melancholy by some favourite air; he would shed tears when I played, and generally wrote some lines afterwards".[15]

And so, listening to the music of the flute and the scratching of Smart's quill, his ageing lungs battling against the apartment's reek of tobacco and wood smoke, venturing out into the streets less and less, Jeoffry continued his life, as the leaves went from green to russet and back again on the south side of St James's Park. Smart had taken to sitting up most of the night, writing by the light of a single candle, while his cat grew old on the armchair beside him. By the spring of 1770 Jeoffry was nineteen, progressively toothless, his skin scabby under his fur, but his ginger coat still bright, and, beneath his eyes, a pentimento of his previous lives. He could see that there were shadows beneath Christopher Smart's eyes dark as bruises. The reek of despair was unmistakable, and Jeoffry trembled in the face of it. The clot of shadows crowded once again around Smart's head, which was wigless and sore. That evening Smart did not eat; he had no appetite, and no money for food. Jeoffry's bowl lay empty, and when his stomach forced him outside (the lethargy of old age can mysteriously disappear from a hungry cat) he found the street had mean pickings for him. Still he dared not approach rats, several of which he saw clumped and nattering in a dark corner. There were few puddles from which to lap, and he ate insects and swiped at moths, raising clouds of dust from the flicker and struggle of their powdered wings. He purred demandingly at passers-by but was shooed away, and returned to the house, finding Smart still in the larger of the two rooms, sitting at his desk, writing, writing. Smart did not pause to stroke Jeoffry, who curled into a ball of hunger in the corner of the room, and resigned himself to sleep.

How the rest of the year played itself out is not known. More of the same, most likely, man and cat eating and sleeping when they could. Christmas went uncelebrated bar Smart's solitary worship, and visitors were few, although Smart's nephew, Christopher Hunter, came occasionally with fish or horse meat for Jeoffry. But Smart himself was paying less and less attention to the cat, and would barely stir or notice when a ginger face pushed itself into the backs of his knees, or when a ginger tail wove around his feet. More often than not Jeoffry was kicked away. At night he would listen to shrieks of pain from the bedstead in the corner of the smaller room, which began to smell of illness and of decay.

Smart's debts were now insurmountable. He faced a trial; it was to come on 11 January 1771. Cats are not allowed in prison, and it is surprising that Jeoffry was not turned out of doors or left to rot in a corner. But by the time Smart was tried by Lord Mansfield and sent to the King's Bench debtors' prison in Southwark, Jeoffry was on his way to Devon.

A lady called Mrs Georgiana Ramm, foaming with lace, her faded gown clearing wide paths through the dust, had visited the rooms with a maidservant specifically to collect Jeoffry. The cat, smelling capture, fearful of the basket, yelled at her from his corner. Smart was sitting at his desk, and the cat shot to him for rescue or reassurance. Smart looked at his cat but did not seem to see him, or even feel him, as Jeoffry pushed his head into the dank and musty cloth of the poet's coat, which was hanging over the back of the wooden chair. With a great effort, he leapt up onto Smart's lap and pushed his proud ageing little body against the familiar chest with all his might. Realising that he was not seen, that he did not seem to be wanted, he gave himself up, was lifted up and away and into a basket lined with straw and cloth for the purpose, and there was no need even to close its lid as he was carried, swaying, silent, out of the life of Christopher Smart.

Jeoffry scrabbled around to get a better purchase, stretched his neck up to see where he was going, and what he was leaving behind. Smart was still sitting, saying something to Mrs Ramm but nothing to Jeoffry. The cat's pupils widened, caught like

large insects in amber. His eyes fastened on Kit
Smart, and they did not let go, even as Smart went
to his desk and began once again to write, even as
the basket shook and spun when the maidservant
transferred her cargo from hand to hand, even as
they left the apartments that had been his home.
His gaze bore through a succession of slammed
doors: the door of their rooms as they clanked down
the stairwell, the door of the house on Park Street,
and the door of Mrs Ramm's carriage. The man left
behind at the desk seemed strangely diminished, as
though there were a little bit less of him left to die.

Jeoffry was soon enough shaken first into panic
and then into sleep, soothed by the provision of
food more plentiful and tasty than anything he
had eaten in some years. But on some days, lying
in her garden in a scrap of sunlight, walking over
Mrs Ramm's desk and feeling the paper beneath
his paws, knocking over the pounce pot and upset-
ting the ink, he felt a pained and unexplained gash
in his quick-beating heart, and thought in a vague

sore way of Kit, whom he had loved. And who, by 20 May 1771, lay dead, of pneumonia, or perhaps of liver failure, or even of tertiary syphilis, in the churchyard of St Paul's in Covent Garden, not far from the cupboard where Jeoffry had been born.

As Jeoffry was bounced south-west in Mrs Ramm's carriage, the manuscript of *Jubilate Agno* lay quite still in Smart's dresser. His nephew, Christopher Hunter, was doubtless given the task of clearing the apartments on his uncle's death. Two years later, in 1773, the poet William Cowper, living in the market town of Olney in Buckinghamshire, experienced an attack of insanity, firm in his belief not only that he was condemned eternally to burn in hell fires, but that God had commanded him to sacrifice his own life, as Abraham had offered his son. Friends watched over him night and day, and after a year he recovered, continuing to live quietly at Olney in the company of his beloved cats, who learned to co-exist amicably with a spaniel and three tame hares, all of them coming and going through a little hatch that had been carved low down in Cowper's front door. The writer William Hayley, with the garrulousness then permitted to biographers, soon embarked on a five-volume biography of Cowper, and, it appears, was somehow sent the manuscript of *Jubilate Agno*, replete with its consideration of Jeoffry. Perhaps it was intended as a case study of madness, an example of the writing produced by an "insane" poetic mind. Cowper's verse quickly settled in the public consciousness; Smart's was more or less dismissed as lunatic ravings, and the manuscript of *Jubilate Agno* was placed in a drawer of the private library in Suffolk of Hayley's friend, the Reverend Thomas Carwardine.

And there it lay, forgotten, undiscovered. The dust gathered in layers over its impassioned and devout calligraphy. Centuries passed. The king went permanently mad; his granddaughter ruled the kingdom for over sixty years; a lattice of railway tracks was laid across the countryside and white crosses sprouted at Flanders Fields in inconceivable multitude. It was not Jeoffry but Hodge who, over the years, became an immortalised literary cat, subject of an elegy by Percival Stockdale and of a statue that sits in Gough Square. He appears in James Boswell's *Life of Samuel Johnson*; in Hester Thrale's *Anecdotes of the Late Samuel Johnson*; and in the *dramatis personae* of an early and unfinished play by Samuel Beckett called *Human Wishes*, which lists three women waiting for Dr Johnson's return alongside "The cat, Hodge (sleeping – if possible)".

Jeoffry would have disappeared into history, were it not for an American diplomat and religious poet named William Force Stead. On 5 March 1938, as Germany was mobilising all along the Austrian border, the *Times Literary Supplement* carried a headline on its front page, not far underneath "Hitler The Early Leader". It read: "A Christopher Smart Manuscript".

William Stead, a few months before, had vis-
ited his friend Colonel W.G. Carwardine Probert,
who was living in the old country house in Suffolk
where once his ancestor the Reverend Thomas
Carwardine had built his library. Stead, poring over
the sixteen folio pages of *Jubilate Agno*, knew he
had found a poem of interest: "Not only Blake, but
such romantic mystics as Coleridge and Shelley
would have been enchanted by some of these
passages. Smart broke through the literary conven-
tions which had dwarfed him and wrote whatever
visited his imagination in whatever words came
most naturally." Stead began to transcribe the
poem and prepare it for publication (although it
would take a later editor to discover that the "Let"
and "For" passages sang to each other in antiphonal
duet). Smart, wrote Stead,

> saw animals magnified as magical beings. In
> one place he writes, "For I am possessed of a
> cat, surpassing in beauty, from whom I take

occasion to bless Almighty God," and there follows a tribute to his cat, Poor Jeoffry, which must take rank as one of the most remarkable poems to a cat ever written.[16]

Stead speedily excerpted the section of *Jubilate Agno* devoted to Jeoffry and, in July 1938, published it in the *Criterion* (a literary magazine edited by no less a figure than T.S. Eliot). And so Jeoffry entered English verse, as the war clouds gathered across Europe.

Stead brought out a complete edition of *Jubilate Agno*, to which he added the rather melodramatic subtitle *A Song from Bedlam*, in the first months of 1939.* Critics greeted it with confusion;

---

* "Bedlam" is strictly the specific hospital of St Mary's Bethlehem in Moorfields, to which Christopher Smart was never sent. Stead (1884–1967) travelled to America a few weeks later, and got stuck there on the outbreak of the Second World War. He was befriended by Tennessee Williams, who immortalised him as the character of Nonno in *The Night of the Iguana* (1961).

subsequent readers found within it a cosmic
radiance to rank with William Blake. Poets from
Wendy Cope to Allen Ginsberg professed Smart
an influence and an inspiration. And Jeoffry,
could he but have known it, had become a poetic
celebrity. Figures of the likes of W.H. Auden
and Edith Sitwell got to know his portrait, and
included him in their influential anthologies. He
appeared in Smart's first *Collected Works*, two small
mustard-coloured volumes running to 1,020 pages,
taken down by the present author from his parents'
shelves, evidently purchased as a gift and inscribed
in black ink ("To Louise, with much love from Ian,
Christmas 1971").

And he was set to music. Semiquavers scamp-
ered and wreathed around him in elegant quickness.
Benjamin Britten's cantata *Rejoice in the Lamb* set
words from Smart's poem, at Auden's sugges-
tion. The piece was first performed at a church in
Northampton, in the pendulous mid-war hush
between the Blitz and the doodlebugs. Jeoffry was

given an aria to himself, for treble solo, much to the concern of the Reverend Walter Hussey, who had commissioned the work and was wary of tweeness. But Britten was certain: "I am afraid I have gone ahead, and used a bit about the cat Jeffrey [*sic*], but I don't see how it could hurt anyone – he is such a nice cat."[17] Five years later, as the country began to rebuild itself, the composer Ruth Gipps devoted to Smart's portrait of Jeoffry the third section of her cantata *The Cat*.

He was illustrated. He was anthologised. He was included in indexes: "Jeoffry, see Smart, Christopher, feline companion". He was, in short, a famous cat. Edith Sitwell wrote of Smart:

There is no room in the heaven of this madman's mind for cruelty or injustice, or for anything but love. That Heaven was undimmed by the cruelties and darkness of prison, unbroken by starvation, warm in the midst of that deathly cold. This madman of

genius, this poet of genius, for all the barriers
of his madness, continued to walk in the cool
of the evening with his God.[18]

Smart had reached for his cat for comfort, bun-
dling him into his ecstatic and infinite vision,
which the world, tiptoeing along on the surface of
life, did not at first understand. Jeoffry had weaved
around his companion's feet as they walked along
the walls of the asylum, between the borders of
carnations, underneath the trees and their angel-
laden branches. Did Jeoffry know Smart's God?
Smart certainly thought so. To agree with him
across the ocean of centuries, on which float ships
of reason and rationality, of evolutionary theory
and of passionate atheism, is a difficult thing, even
as the devout continue to preach from the shore.
But cats, we may say, are aware of more things in
heaven and earth than are dreamt of in our narrow
human philosophy. And it is certain that, mad or
sane, Kit Smart, in the visible darkness of his life,

was possessed of a cat, surpassing in beauty, and
this too is god.

6

THE END

1770–1773

The journey to Devon, braved in the last weeks of 1770, took four days. Mrs Ramm had once been wealthy. These days she lived on the dwindling income of her second widowhood, and could not run to the expense of a well-sprung carriage; the liveries of her coachmen were patched at the elbows. Jeoffry was in his basket on the floor, and each day, as it bounced and rattled and bumped its way across the fraying carpet, he yowled without cease, alternately wetting himself, so that the stinking liquid ran through the wicker and onto the floor, and vomiting, with the hacking melodrama peculiar to cats. The freezing conveyance thundered its way along cobbles, and Mrs Ramm, bundled in furs, cursed her generosity of spirit. Her maid, Maggie, held a handkerchief to her face and wondered why on earth they were bothering to transport this wretched animal hundreds of miles across country. They spent the nights at inns while the driver rested and the horses were changed, and Jeoffry was put in Maggie's cheap attic room. She dutifully carried him out into the icy garden each evening, but barely let him go, lest he scamper into the undergrowth and disappear. One of Mrs Ramm's coachmen took a shine to the cat, rather bemused by his mistress's eccentric decision to haul the elderly ginger animal back to Devon in a basket, and saved him scraps from his own meal. Innkeepers sent them off with hot water poured into copper bottles and wrapped in muslin, which they held close.

Quite why Mrs Georgiana Ramm had taken the elderly cat back to her house in Devon is uncertain. Had she known Jeoffry's true age, which his sprightliness hid from strangers, she might have sent him to a local farrier for speedy despatch. She was devoutly religious and quietly literary, and had once asked Dr Johnson a question at Hester Thrale's dinner table which had been answered at length; perhaps she had accepted Jeoffry in the spirit of a fan purchasing a keepsake from a writer she admired. Perhaps, a distant friend of Christopher Hunter and genuinely upset at Smart's plight, she had decided to do a good turn. Perhaps she adored cats.

She lived at the small market town of Ottery St Mary, in a house of faded grandeur that was held in trust for her lifetime and would eventually pass to the eldest of her many children. The carriage turned off the London-to-Exeter road and drove towards the sea. The soil turned maroon, and the three of them eventually bumped their way first along a track bordered with hedges and then through the narrow roads of Ottery St Mary and its jumble of honey-coloured houses. Jeoffry had arrived at his last home, although it took him many days to acclimatise himself to the shabby, disused rooms, and not to flinch at the torrent of bells that rang each day from the great tower at St Mary's.

Mrs Ramm passed her mornings writing lengthy and detailed letters to a close relation living in Buckinghamshire. Jeoffry – which she spelled differently to Smart, always calling him "Geoffrey" – is not frequently mentioned in her correspondence, but he appears enough for links to be made, for his journey from London to Devon to be narrated, and for his story to be sketchily continued and completed. "Did I tell you of Mr Smart the poet?" Mrs Ramm wrote:

> Twice confined in a madhouse after some strange afflixion of mind, he has been taken finally into a debtor's prison – and through a strange con-cat-enation (!) of circumstances that I shall not bore you with dearest, 'tis fallen to me to look after his beloved cat Geoffrey in his final years. This I am happy to do, as I am sure the animal will be a good companion for me, although at the moment we are very mistrustful of each other after the long journey from London, which I do hate to visit. But I feel sure we shall become friends. He seems a dear creature, & a prettier cat you never saw, all over stripes, & the colour of autumn leaves.

Mrs Ramm maintained a respectable position in the town, despite her financial vicissitudes. There had been some talk, when she was growing up, of her being painted by Gainsborough, and remnants of her beauty still crept, every now and then, to the surface of her ravaged and powdered skin. She was nearing fifty-five, her hair faded and feathery beneath her wig, her joints tired of life. Her daughters had not married as well as she might have liked; her sons were a various and predictable clutch of vicars, doctors, farmers, and soldiers. One of them was to die in the American Revolutionary War, shot instantly dead on the North Bridge in Concord. She ate her small Christmas bird alone, and afterwards took a glass of sherry with Maggie in the kitchen.

Jeoffry was soon to reach the great age of twenty-one. He was well preserved, occasionally energetic, and seemingly in good health. In that first spring of his Devon retirement, disarmed by yet another change in his fortunes, he would frisk suddenly

through Mrs Ramm's garden, and although the
wall that surrounded it, drenched in creeper, was
now of sadly insurmountable height for him, he
soon realised that he could push against a rotting
wooden door and nose his way through long grass
into the graveyard of the church. The sea, churn-
ing onto the peaty Devon coast at Sidmouth just
six miles to the south, had filled the air and the rain
with an exotic tang, strange and unidentifiable.

For a while the gravestones were an intriguing
sculpture park, of cool seats and reeking moss. But
one morning Mrs Ramm stooped to stroke him
and realised that, almost overnight it seemed, her
cat had become very old. His coat was still flecked
a hundred colours, very few of them grey. But there
was a stiffness in his back legs now as he cultivated a
kind of graceful lollop through Mrs Ramm's house,
and he was soon content to sit quietly through the
days, sinking into the long grass of the garden in
summer, and steamrollered across the floor in front
of the range in winter. The tips of his whiskers had

a frayed look, and there was something indefinably old about his face, some mournful grizzle around the nose and mouth that led what few visitors Mrs Ramm had to stroke his head with an especial gentleness. He purred mightily at this, articulate as ever.

His age seems to have caught him in a strange stasis. His coat matted, and his eyes became rheumy, but his slow-working body halted the progress of any otherwise-fatal illness. It was 1771, and Jeoffry took up daily residence on a small footstool that Mrs Ramm had embroidered with coiling sprays of lily-of-the-valley. It was 1772, and Maggie grew used to checking the footstool each morning to see that the cat was still breathing. Just before Christmas of that year, Mrs Ramm was honoured with a visit from the church's vicar, John Coleridge, and his wife, Anne. Mrs Ramm instructed Maggie to use three spoonfuls of the precious tin of tea leaves that usually sat untouched on the dresser. They drank it together in the parlour, using the best china, with the cat wheezing on the footstool. None of them was able to tell which end of him was which, so tightly had he curled himself into the lily-of-the-valley, but each was imbued with the curious calm that a sleeping cat can bring to a room.

The Coleridges' youngest child, Sam, a handful of months old, was in his mother's arms. He was a large baby, his dimpled rubbery limbs and black hair poking from his white dress, a fist holding tightly on to his mother's little finger. His eyes were large, lamplit, of a strange unknowable grey, and they gazed down at the cat sleeping beneath him. The vicar liked cats and, unaware of Jeoffry's age, bent down to scoop him up. Jeoffry made a strange yowl, and the vicar put him hurriedly onto the pink sofa. The vicar's wife, carefully holding up her son's head, leant down so that the baby could look at the cat, and the baby stuck out an arm so that his tiny fingers and their impossibly small nails just brushed through Jeoffry's coat, and the cat made a rattling noise that might have been a purr. And all the while nobody knew that Jeoffry had once danced in the rain with Christopher Smart, and nearly died in the 'flu-ridden fug of a lunatic asylum. Nobody guessed that he had paced with Nancy along the thick carpets of London's most infamous whorehouse, or watched Hugh Collins's mother weep as her son went off to sea with his cat under his arm. All the cats that he had been, all the lives he had led, in solitude and companionship, amid joy and madness and loss, seemed quietly to meld amid the smell of the tea leaves, and the silver clink of their pastry forks.

That Christmas was exceptionally cold, and Jeoffry was carried gently into the kitchen and placed on a mat in front of the range. The snow carpeted the green lawn outside, and Mrs Ramm took her embroidery into the kitchen and chatted to Maggie as she brushed the top of a pie with egg yolk. Jeoffry pressed his nose into the range. The bells of St Mary's rang in 1773.

There was a muffle at the edge of Jeoffry's hearing, and he no longer scuffled towards the ringing of pottery on flagstone, as a bowl of scraps or dish of water was put down for him. The meat curled and greyed and went untouched, although he would dutifully lick off the gravy. His standards remained high, and he would mew at the back door to be let out into the garden twice a night, rain or shine, snow or dew, and leave a scatter of muddy prints as he hobbled back through the kitchen. But he was twenty-two: a great age for a cat. The lights in his coat were going out, and his eyes were milky, staring at Mrs Ramm from behind a thin pained film of unseeing. And his hind legs grew yet more stiff. More than once Mrs Ramm, running her liver-spotted hand along the ridges of Jeoffry's spine and finding his bones like railings beneath the scrub of his fur, thought of asking one of her younger sons to bring a gun for him, from the farm. But never quite asked.

Nor, in the end, had she need. Some time in the first months of the year, as Mrs Ramm was looking out at the snowdrops pricking through the soil of her garden, she heard a faint mew, guttural, guttering. She looked down to see Jeoffry slinking slowly across the carpet, stomach to the ground. He had not tolerated more than the briefest touch for some days, but consented, on this chill and sunlit morning, to be lifted onto her lap as she bundled the two of them onto a sofa. The memory of skirts and comforters was a distant one to him. He drew a faint outline of a thought, a distant recollection of Nancy, her pungent and rather slapdash kindness, the glorious resistance and then give of her spun silk, catching delightfully beneath his claws. Now, he merely pushed his head into the balled fist of Mrs Ramm. She felt his nose cold and dry as it found the crevice beneath her fingers and settled there. Her rings, shabby and scratched now, but the stones still lustrous in their cheap setting, were cool against his face. He was trembling slightly, his sides billowing in and out, slightly distended. But he made no attempt to move, and she sat still, calm and expectant, and let him manage his dying as he wished. She had held the hand of her two husbands on their deathbeds, one liked, one utterly beloved; and had seen two of her babies, mangled and twisted, taken from her like unwanted parcels, wrapped in a white sheet. A third child, three years old, had released a tight grip on her finger as he succumbed to some as-yet-unnamed illness, something rattling and boiling in his chest. She knew death, knew its sound and its atmosphere, and was calm in its presence.

A biographer cannot know his subject's dying thoughts, merely recount Jeoffry's "slight wheeze", described by Mrs Ramm in a brisk postscript to a letter for her friend, Mrs Coleridge, the vicar's wife. As Jeoffry pressed closer to the arthritic bunches of knuckle, Mrs Ramm's hand, skinned of its glove, was perhaps his focus; or perhaps he had no focus. Likely he had no thought of his Kit, nor of Nancy and old Mother Douglas, the three now lying, unnamed and unmourned, in paupers' graves. The cat twitched slightly to a clank of pots from Maggie in the kitchen. Mrs Ramm sat on, still as stone, breathing only as he breathed, waiting patiently amid the floral wallpaper and the clock's ticking and the quiet tearing of soul from body. She thought of the patch in the garden, beneath the snowdrops, where she would ask her youngest and most devoted son to bury him, and of the simple gravestone that she might ask Mr Seaton to make, assuming the price was not too dear. Today, in one corner of the garden at the back of the house, is a mossy tablet, inscribed: "Geoffrey. Requiescat."

The grey fuzz at the edges of the cat's vision spread slowly inward. His fur was suddenly unconnected to his body, which was still and quiet. Just that. Nothing sweeter than his peace when at rest.

AFTERWORD

My debt to Virginia Woolf's *Flush: A Biography* (London: Hogarth Press, 1933) will be obvious. I would like also to acknowledge my grateful reliance upon the following books:

Ainsworth, Edward G., and Noyes, Charles E., *Christopher Smart: A Biographical and Critical Study* (Columbia: University of Missouri Press, 1943).

Dearnley, Moira, *The Poetry of Christopher Smart* (London: Routledge & Kegan Paul, 1968).

Devlin, Christopher, *Poor Kit Smart* (London: Rupert Hart-Davis, 1961).

Frayling, Christopher, *Horace Walpole's Cat* (London: Thames & Hudson, 2009).

Holmes, Richard, *Coleridge: Early Visions* (London: Hodder & Stoughton, 1989).

Mounsey, Chris, *Clown of God* (Lewisburg: Bucknell University Press, 2001).

Rizzo, Betty, and Mahony, Robert, *The Annotated Letters of Christopher Smart* (Carbondale: Southern Illinois University Press, 1991).

Rubenhold, Hallie, *The Covent Garden Ladies: Pimp General Jack and the Extraordinary Story of "Harris's List"* (Stroud: Tempus, 2005).

Sherbo, Arthur, *Christopher Smart, Scholar of the University* (East Lansing: Michigan State University Press, 1967).

Williamson, Karina, *The Poetical Works of Christopher Smart – I. Jubilate Agno* (Oxford: Clarendon Press, 1980).

Nancy's diaries and life are imaginary, but her entry in Mr Harris's list for 1761 is not. Hugh Collins and his life, Mrs Ramm and hers, are invention. The Coleridges and their baby are not.

Beyond what Smart wrote about his beloved cat in *Jubilate Agno*, nothing is known about Jeoffry, although it is generally agreed, given the auto-biographical and even diary-like nature of the poem, that he existed, and did not frolic only within Smart's verse. So my portrait of the cat, and of his life, is imaginary. But that seems to me no reason for it not to be true.

ACKNOWLEDGEMENTS

My thanks to my agent, Ian Drury at Sheil Land, and to my editor, Simon Wright at The History Press, for believing this book was something more than a curio. Simon, and the copy-editor, Catherine Hanley, proceeded with a care and scrupulousness that saved me from many a howler, not least the methods of eighteenth-century capital punishment and the duration of a cat's pregnancy. I am grateful to all at The History Press for looking after Jeoffry so well, and taking him so seriously. Nicholas Clark and Simon Learmount offered kind assistance.

I am fortunate in having friends and family who either share or tolerate my devotion to cats, and many of them were among my early and most valued readers: Eileen Atkins; Sally Groves; Thérèse Oulton and Peter Gidal; Jill Paton Walsh; Roger Savage; Ruth Smith; Louise and Ian Soden; Elizabeth Tregear.

The cats in my life (Henry and Stanley of blessed memory; Maud and – inevitably – Jeoffry) have borne nobly my helpless adoration. And to Yrja Thorsdottir love and thanks, always.

NOTES

The reader can be assured that all the following are *bona fide*.

THE POEM

musk   In this instance, likely a form of geranium (see Keats's "Isabella": "close in a bower of hyacinth and musk"); or perhaps a small fruit, thrown in play (i.e. musk apple). See, elsewhere in *Jubilate Agno*:

"Let Magpiash rejoice with the Musk" (C161, with "musk" variously glossed, in editions of the poem, as a geranium, a grass … and a cat).

upon the beat   Smart's use of the phrase perplexed the first annotators of *Jubilate Agno*, for there then existed no record in English of a "beat" being used to refer to the habitual rounds of a watchman or constable, surely the sense here, prior to 1825. The *Oxford English Dictionary* has more recently traced an example of this usage from 1721.

For the Lord commanded Moses concerning the cats

Alas, He didn't. Cats are not mentioned in the Protestant Bible.

in the bag   The phrase "to let the cat out of the
                    bag", meaning to disclose a secret,
                    was in common usage when Smart
                    wrote *Jubilate Agno*.

spraggle upon waggle
                    "Spraggle": a Scots word mean-
                    ing "flail" or "sprawl" (usually
                    "sprauchle"); "waggle": seemingly
                    referring to a wagging finger.

camels   Presumably "humps" or "arches" (a
                    unique coinage).

Ichneumon-rat The Ichneumon, actually a species
                    of mongoose, was in truth vener-
                    ated by the Egyptians for, like cats,
                    preying upon rodents and snakes.

sting   In the sense of "tingle" (*Oxford English Dictionary*).

electricity   Not only a description of the static charge in Jeoffry's fur or of the electrical hum of his purring, but evidence of the eighteenth-century notion that cats generated electricity. See an anonymous article in *Gentleman's Magazine*, Vol. 29 (1754), pp. 112–13:

Natural electricity is common almost to all animals, especially those destin'd to catch their prey by night; cats have this property in the greatest degree of any animal we are acquainted with; their furr or hair is surprizingly electrical. If it be gently raised up it avoids the touch till it be forc'd to it, and by stroking their backs in the dark, the emanations of electrical fire are extremely quick and vibrative from it, follow'd by a crackling noise as from glass tubes when their electrical atmosphere is struck. It appears to me of singular use to animals destin'd to catch their prey in the dark; they give a sudden and quick erection to their furr, which raises the electrical fire, and this, by its quickness rushing along the long pointed hairs over their eyes, and illuminating the pupilla enables them to perceive and seize their prey.

CHAPTER 1

1 London's earthquake-induced panic in spring 1750 is vividly described, although misdated, in Charles Mackay, *Memoirs of Extraordinary Popular Delusions and the Madness of Crowds* (London: Office of the National Illustrated Library, 1852), p. 224.

CHAPTER 2

2 See Heather McPherson, "Theatrical Riots and Cultural Politics in Eighteenth-Century London", *The Eighteenth Century*, Vol. 43, No. 3 (Fall 2002), pp. 236–52.

3 The raids of summer 1758 on the Covent Garden bordellos are brilliantly documented in Hallie Rubenhold, *The Covent Garden Ladies: Pimp General Jack and the Extraordinary Story of "Harris's List"* (Stroud: Tempus, 2005).

4 *Harris's List of Covent Garden Ladies: Sex in the City in Georgian Britain*, ed. by Hallie Rubenhold (Stroud: Tempus, 2005), p. 154.

CHAPTER 3

5 James Boswell, *The Life of Samuel Johnson*, 1791 (New York: Alfred A. Knopf, 1992), p. 250.

6 Quoted in Christopher Devlin, *Poor Kit Smart* (London: Rupert Hart-Davis, 1961), p. 101.

7 Reported by Mrs Thrale, and quoted by Devlin in *Poor Kit Smart*, p. 116. Devlin settles for Turlington's House; most other accounts for Mr Potter's, in Bethnal Green.

8 Although it is generally agreed that Smart's treatment in the asylum was not excessively cruel, Chris Mounsey explores the darker side of his confinement in *Clown of God* (Lewisburg: Bucknell University Press, 2001), pp. 204–6.

9 The use on Smart of an instrument by which he was force-fed medicine is suggested by Karina

Williamson in her edition of *The Poetical Works of Christopher Smart – I. Jubilate Agno* (Oxford: Clarendon Press, 1980), p. 32n.

CHAPTER 4

10 "It seems possible that sending patients out naked in the rain was a typical method of keeping them clean." Mounsey, *Clown of God*, p. 208.

11 "1762. Sir George Baker commences his relation by saying, that on April 4, three persons were attacked in the same house by the same disease; and by April 24 it had spread through the whole of London. It attacked all indiscriminately, and was fatal to the aged, and particularly to those who were asthmatic. The burials in the bill for the week ending May 4, were 467, and for the weeks following, 626, 750, 659, 516, 504." "Previous Epidemics of Influenza in England", *Journal of the Statistical Society*

of London – Vol. XI (London: John William Parker, 1848), p. 173.

CHAPTER 5

12 The conversation is taken verbatim from Boswell, *Samuel Johnson*, p. 250.

13 *The Early Journals and Letters of Fanny Burney, Volume One, 1768–1773* (Oxford: Clarendon Press, 1988), p. 36. To allow Fanny Burney and Jeoffry the pleasure of each other's company I have altered the location of the meeting, which actually took place at the Burneys' household.

14 *Early Journals and Letters of Fanny Burney*, p. 91.

15 Quoted in Devlin, *Poor Kit Smart*, p. 185.

16 W. Force Stead, "A Christopher Smart Manuscript", *Times Literary Supplement*, 5 March 1938, p. 152.

17 *Letters from a Life: Selected Letters and Diaries of Benjamin Britten: Volume Two, 1939–45,*

ed. by Donald Mitchell and Philip Reed (London: Faber & Faber, 1991), p. 1157.

18 Edith Sitwell, *The Pleasures of Poetry*, First Series (London: Duckworth, 1930).

INDEX

catches influenza 114–15; leaves asylum for lodgings on Park Street 119–20; newfound freedom 120–1; meets Hodge 122; life in the Park Street apartments 126–7, 131–3; meets Fanny Burney 127–9; hears flautist 130–1; departure from Park Street 134–6; immortality in British literature 141–3; travels to Devon 147–9; life at Ottery St Mary 151–3; in poor health, 152–3; meets Samuel Taylor Coleridge 154–5; in great old age 156; death 157–9; monument 159

Appearance: eyes 25; coat 6–7, 39, 131, 152, 153, 156; paws 7, 22; tail 7, 70, 133; whiskers 7, 101–2, 152–3

Character and characteristics: affection 25, 91; cleanliness 12, 39, 101; diet 100, 112, 133; fighting instincts 36–7, 40; health 60, 151, 153; hearing 33, 43, 45; hunting instincts 39–40, 49, 100, 132; playfulness 110, 128; sense of smell 24, 31, 36; sex life 41; street wisdom 121; superiority 34; toilet habits 12, 100, 156; vision 5–6, 156

Relationships: with other cats 35–7, 39, 41, 122; with Fanny Burney 127–9; with Nancy Burroughs 10–11, 24–6, 37–40, 55–6, 157; with David Garrick 42, 50, 77, 109;